Body of State

The Fairleigh Dickinson University Press Series In Italian Studies

General Editor: Dr. Anthony Julian Tamburri, Dean, John D. Calandra Italian American Institute (Queens College-CUNY)

The Fairleigh Dickinson University Press Series in Italian Studies is devoted to the publication of scholarly works on Italian literature, film, history, biography, art, and culture, as well as on intercultural connections, such as Italian-American Studies.

Recent Publications in Italian Studies

Marini-Maio, Nicoletta, Ellen Nerenberg, and Thomas Simpson (trans.), Marco Baliani, *Body of State* (2012)

Godey, Amber R., *Sister Souls: The Power of Personal Narrative in the Poetic Works of Antonia Pozzi and Vittorio Sereni* (2011)

Verdicchio, Pasquale, *Looters, Photographers, and Thieves: Aspects of Italian Photographic Culture in the Nineteenth and Twentieth Centuries* (2011)

Parati, Graziella, and Anthony Julian Tamburri (eds.), *The Cultures of Italian Migration* (2011)

Trubiano, Marisa S., *Ennio Flaiano and His Italy: Postcards from a Changing World* (2010)

Halliday, Iain, *Huck Finn in Italian, Pinocchio in English: Theory and Praxis of Literary Translation* (2009)

Serram, Ilaria, *The Imagined Immigrant: The Images of Italian Emigration to the United States between 1890 and 1924* (2009)

Lucamante, Stefania, ed., *Italy and the Bourgeoisie: The Re-Thinking of a Class* (2009)

Van Order, Thomas, *Listening to Fellini: Music and Meaning in Black and White* (2008)

Billiani, Francesca, and Gigliola Sulis, *The Italian Gothic and Fantastic: Encounters and Rewritings of Narrative Traditions* (2008)

Orton, Marie, and Graziella Parati (eds.), *Multicultural Literature in Contemporary Italy* (2007)

Scambray, Ken, *Queen Calafia's Paradise: California and the Italian-American Novel* (2007)

Polezzi, Loredana, and Charlotte Ross (eds.), *In Corpore: Bodies in Post-Unification Italy* (2007)

Francese, Joseph, *Socially Symbolic Acts: The Historicizing Fictions of Umberto Eco, Vincenzo Consolo, and Antonio Tabucchi* (2006)

Kozma, Jan (trans.), Grazia Deledda, *Marianna Sirca* (2006)

On the Web at http://www.fdu.edu/fdupress

Body of State

The Moro Affair, a Nation Divided

Marco Baliani

**Translated by Nicoletta Marini-Maio,
Ellen Nerenberg, and Thomas Simpson**

**Critical Introduction by
Nicoletta Marini-Maio
and Ellen Nerenberg**

Fairleigh Dickinson

FAIRLEIGH DICKINSON UNIVERSITY PRESS
Madison • Teaneck

Published by Fairleigh Dickinson University Press
Co-published with The Rowman & Littlefield Publishing Group, Inc.
4501 Forbes Boulevard, Suite 200, Lanham, Maryland 20706
www.rowmanlittlefield.com

Estover Road, Plymouth PL6 7PY, United Kingdom

British Library Cataloguing in Publication Information Available

Library of Congress Cataloging-in-Publication Data
Baliani, Marco, 1950–
  [Corpo di stato. English]
  Body of state : the Moro affair, a nation divided / by Marco Baliani ; translated by
Nicoletta Marini-Maio, Ellen Nerenberg, and Thomas Simpson ; critical introduction by
Nicoletta Marini-Maio and Ellen Nerenberg.
    p. cm. — (The Fairleigh Dickinson University Press series in Italian studies)
  Includes index.
  ISBN 978-1-61147-463-3 (cloth : alk. paper) — ISBN 978-1-61147-464-0 (ebook)
  1. Moro, Aldo, 1916–1978—Kidnapping, 1978—Drama. 2. Moro, Aldo, 1916–1978—
Assassination—Drama. 3. Brigate rosse—Drama. 4. Terrorism—Italy—Drama. 5. Italy—
Politics and government—1976–1994—Drama. 6. Monologues, Italian—Translations
into English. 7. Baliani, Marco, 1950– —Criticism and interpretation. 8. Baliani, Marco,
1950– —Diaries. 9. Baliani, Marco, 1950– —Interviews. I. Marini-Maio, Nicoletta,
1961– II. Nerenberg, Ellen Victoria, 1962– III. Title.
  PQ4862.A374C6713 2012
  852'.92—dc23   2011034189

♾TM The paper used in this publication meets the minimum requirements of American
National Standard for Information Sciences—Permanence of Paper for Printed Library
Materials, ANSI/NISO Z39.48-1992.

Printed in the United States of America

Contents

Preface

HISTORICAL MEMORY AS
THEATRICAL MONTAGE

Ron Jenkins

> Montage in the theater is linked to the ability that an actor
> or director has to use the movie camera that every specta-
> tor has unknowingly installed in his brain . . . even before
> the invention of modern cinematographic technology,
> all talented actors succeeded in utilizing the technique of
> the movie camera to give sensitive spectators the illusion
> of close-ups and reaction shots and even long shots with
> wide-angle panorama.
>
> —Dario Fo[1]

Marco Baliani cites Dario Fo as one of his sources of inspiration, and the television director Felice Cappa, who orchestrated the broadcast of Baliani's *Body
of State* on the RAI network in Italy, has also televised many of Fo's performances. As he does for Fo, Cappa creates a montage of shifting camera angles
that enhances the complex textual and gestural montage already inherent in
Baliani's live performance. In the case of *Body of State* Cappa deepens the
resonance of the play's references to recent history by placing it in an ancient
historical setting, the Roman Forum. Baliani, performing alone without props
or costumes, uses his body and voice to conjure up images of the 1978 kidnapping and assassination of Aldo Moro and other acts of political violence from
that turbulent era of Italy's past. Riots. Bombings. Police beating demonstrators. Demonstrators throwing rocks at the police. His deft use of gesture creates an emotional montage that personalizes the newsreel blitz of public events.
Uncertain trembling hands clench slowly into fists of anger. Bystanders cross
themselves as they witness acts of police brutality. Activists raise their arms to
signal their willingness to become *clandestini*, underground operatives who

burn their identity cards and commit themselves to a nomadic existence of armed resistance against the government. Moving from long shots of historic moments to intimate close-ups of his personal reactions, Baliani uses simple gestures to create an emotional montage that ranges from euphoria, outrage, and fear to uncertainty, shame, and confusion. He is most compelling when depicting the psychological paralysis of impossible choices. He stands in a doorway, unable to step back and invite in an old friend for fear of being implicated as an accomplice in the terrorist acts she has committed. He is equally unable to close the door on her. The actor's immobility pauses the montage, allowing the focus to zoom in on a frozen frame of moral anguish.

Another striking moment in Baliani's kinetic sequence emerges when he gestures behind himself as a way of going backward through time, inviting the audience to compare Moro's kidnapping to past acts of violence, like the bombings of Piazza Fontana, when right-wing extremists colluded with government agents to commit terrorist acts and blame them on the Left.[2] This gesturing toward the past is echoed by the landscape in which Baliani performs, an ancient ruin littered with fragments of history. The crumbling columns behind Baliani are pregnant markers of Rome's political heritage. The fallen Forum is a reminder of a fledgling pseudo-democracy that could not sustain itself. The camera shifts angles suggestively to heighten the viewer's awareness of these historic ruins, and at the end of the play, when Baliani recounts the discovery of Moro's dead body, the camera pans upward, leaving the actor and his audience out of the picture for a slow pan of the site's scarred stone walls, as if civilization has vanished from our era as it had in ancient Rome. Crackling voices from old news broadcasts and police bulletins provide a soundtrack that superimposes the past over the present. At this point the montage is technological, but it reinforces the impression made by the swirling montage of Baliani's text and gestures: historical memory and personal recollection bleed into one another in ways that are ever present but often forgotten.

While Italian audiences might compare Baliani's virtuosity as a solo performer to the montage techniques of Dario Fo, his style might be more aptly linked to the less pyrotechnic but equally virtuosic performance style of the late American performance artist Spalding Gray. Gray, like Fo and Baliani, mastered the art of theatrical montage, showering his audiences with memories that were structured like a film full of jump cuts, reactions shots, and changing points of view. His most acclaimed stage performance, *Swimming to Cambodia*, was filmed by Jonathan Demme, who echoed Gray's cinematic techniques in the movement of his camera, doing for the American performer what Cappa did for Fo and Baliani. The parallel goes further in the case of *Swimming to Cambodia*, which is a loose account of Gray's political awakening as he was playing a small role in *The Killing Fields*, a film about the Vietnam War. Sitting behind a desk for the entire performance, Gray's subtle gestures are miniaturized compared to Fo's, much more comparable to the low-key style of Baliani, which erupts only occasionally into full-bodied physical action. (Both Gray and Baliani coincidentally use whirling arm movements to suggest the arrival of helicopters.)

Where Gray and Baliani are most alike is in their shrewd interweaving of personal memories with public events that the audience can associate with their own memories of the past. In Gray's performance, the montage of private recollections with recent history is filtered through the collective memory of the mass media. He artfully alters the techniques of a newspaper reporter to tell the story of a war most Americans remember through television broadcasts as he reenacted it in a film. Baliani also structures his memory montage with reference to the mass media. In the intervals between his play's scenes, Baliani projects black-and-white photographs of demonstrations, riots, and politicians that recall old newspaper clippings (though many of them have, in fact, never been published). They are accompanied by a soundtrack that sounds like archival radio broadcasts. In the RAI television broadcast of *Body of State*, Baliani and Cappa juxtapose these modern mass media techniques with ancient forms of public communication, like Latin inscriptions on stone pillars. The time-worn engravings visible behind Baliani in the Roman Forum suggest both the endurance and the fragility of democracy. The inscriptions have survived centuries of erosion, but their traces are preserved in fragments of a dead language that few can read.

Spalding Gray called himself a "poetic reporter," a performer who was "more like an impressionist painter than a photographer." He described the difference like this: "Most reporters get the facts out as quickly as possible—fresh news is the best news. I do just the opposite. I give the facts a chance to settle down until at last they blend, bubble and mix in the swamp of dream, memory and reflection."[3] Baliani might also be termed a "poetic reporter," an impressionist painter of memory montage who invites audiences to dredge up new meanings from the swamp of their own private and public pasts.

This translation of Baliani's work captures the impressionistic and kinetic spirit of his vision. English-speaking readers are treated to a well-edited montage of texts, notes, and videos that draw them into the whirlwind of memory, fact, and fiction that constitute Baliani's theater at its best. The volume begins with a dramatically energetic translation of *Body of State* that jumps frenetically from a photo of Moro "with that white cowlick in his hair" to "the funerals for Moro's five bodyguards," to an argument on a beach about *Moby Dick* as "a sort of sacred book," to prison visits with "pale and worn-out" revolutionaries, to children's theater performances in which the heroine Petrosinella "has successfully freed herself from jail." The script makes evocative references to old photographs, newspaper articles, and personal address books as it leaps through multiple time frames, and shifts focus from individual lives to political movements with dizzying virtuosity.

The precise clarity of this English language version beautifully conveys the intimate documentary style of the original Italian.

Not only is the text of *Body of State* translated in a way that is faithful to its cinematic structure, but the script is also presented in the context of other elements that enhance the reader's experience of documentary montage. The translation of *Body of State* is followed by Baliani's diary of the television production, linking it to *Antigone delle città*, the work he staged to commemorate the right-wing terrorist bombings that took place in Bologna in 1980. Like Baliani, the reader can take a mental journey from ancient Greece to modern Italy, juxtaposing images of Antigone's defiance of Creon's tyranny against images of the Red Brigades' defiance of Italy's Christian Democrats.

The volume also includes Baliani's reflections on his American tour of *Body of State,* enabling readers to superimpose yet another set of political circumstances on the ever-changing interpretation of the play. A transcribed interview with Baliani about his work provides an informal counterpoint to the theatricality of the written texts. The book is annotated throughout with valuable notes that provide essential background information, and fuel for further speculation about the changing frames of reference employed by Baliani in his theater.

For English-speaking readers this wisely edited and compellingly translated montage of text, counter-text, context, and text-in-performance is an invaluable introduction to the impressionistic poetic reporting of an important Italian performer whose cinematic style transforms history into art.

Notes

1. Dario Fo, *Manuale Minimo Dell'Attore* (Turin: Einaudi, 1987), 190, quoted and translated in Ron Jenkins, *Artful Laughter* (New York: Aperture, 2001), 45.

2. See the introduction of this book for an explanation of the 1969 bombing of the Banca Nazionale di Agricoltura in Milan's Piazza Fontana.

3. Ron Jenkins, *Acrobats of the Soul: Comedy & Virtuosity in Contemporary American Theatre* (New York: Theater Communications Group, 1988), 123.

Acknowledgments

There are many people who assisted the 2009 North American tour of *Corpo di Stato*, which was the genesis of this project. Those deserving of thanks include Stefano Albertini and the staff at New York University's Casa Italiana Zerilli-Marimò, Sandra Carletti, Millicent Marcus, Colleen Ryan, Rita Venturelli and the staff of the Italian Cultural Institute in Washington, Mary Wood, and Tina Cervone and the staff at the Italian Cultural Institute of Chicago.

Special thanks are extended to many members of the staff and colleagues of Dickinson College, Northwestern University, and Wesleyan University, for their unflagging assistance in funding, designing, and organizing Marco Baliani and Maria Maglietta's 2009 tour. We thank the Central Pennsylvania Consortium, Sherry and Kevin Harper-McCombs of Dickinson's Department of Theater and Dance, Nancy Mellersky of Dickinson's Film Studies Program, the staff and colleagues of the Department of French and Italian (particularly Paola Bonifazio and Adele Sanna), and Tom Smith of Dickinson's Media Center. We are grateful to the staff at Wesleyan's Center for the Arts (particularly Barbara Ally and Bob Russo), to Claudia Nascimento of Wesleyan's Theater Department, to Wesleyan's Department of Romance Languages and Literatures, the Catharine and Thomas McMahon Fund, and to Sergei Bunaev, Grace Kredell, Andrea Travertino, and Daniela Viale. We likewise wish to thank the Department of French and Italian at Northwestern University and its chair, Jane Winston.

We are grateful to Wesleyan's John Wareham for assistance with preparation of the artwork for this volume. We also thank the staff of the Multimedia Learning Center at Northwestern University, especially Cecile Sison, Mark Schaefer, and Matthew Taylor, who filmed the event and provided the performance photos in this volume. We offer thanks to Anthony Tamburri and Harry Key-ishian at Fairleigh-Dickinson University Press and to our anonymous reader for the thoughtful and meaningful critique.

The authors would particularly like to thank their partners for the constancy and support they have shown: Rita Filanti, Vittorio Maio, and Anthony Valerio.

Above all, we would like to thank Marco Baliani and Maria Maglietta for their vision, commitment, patience, and availability.

CHAPTER 1

Critical Introduction

CORPSES AND COUPS: ON *BODY OF STATE*

Nicoletta Marini-Maio and Ellen Nerenberg

Where were you when you heard that John F. Kennedy was shot? Or his brother, Robert Kennedy? Or the Reverend Martin Luther King Jr.? Or when you heard that Egyptian president Anwar Sadat had been assassinated? Or Indira Ghandi? Assuming any of these assassinations of state or ideologically inflected murders marked a specific moment in your life, what do you think of when you reflect back on that time? How does one measure the various distances—political, historical, cultural, emotional, psychological—from the you of that moment to the you of this one? Using the cataclysmic event in Italy of the 1978 kidnapping, sequester, and eventual assassination of Aldo Moro by the terrorist organization the Red Brigades (BR), the narrator of Marco Baliani's *Body of State* attempts just this sort of assessment.

As the writer Italo Calvino suggested, the personal story of any individual is linked to wider historical context. "History is made up of little, anonymous gestures," he wrote, adding that "I may die tomorrow even before that German, but everything I do before dying and my death, too, will be little parts of history and all the thoughts I'm having now will influence my history tomorrow, tomorrow's history of the human race."[1] Calvino wrote this in the confusion of the immediate aftermath of World War II. He felt an urgency to share his own experience as a partisan in the civil war in Italy (1941–1943) after the fall of fascism. Like Calvino, the theatrical narrator of *Body of State* also tells his own story against the background of a period characterized by social and political turmoil—that is, the 1970s, the *anni di piombo*, or the so-called years of lead, as this chapter of political terrorism in Italy is known. For Baliani, and, with him, the generation of young Italian people from fifteen to thirty in the decade beginning in 1968, the event is not an experience of war like Calvino's. Moro's kidnapping, sequester, and assassination constitute the cataclysmic experience against which all subsequent events are measured and weighed, compared and contrasted.

Baliani's theater locks firmly onto the coordinates of art and society, theater and politics. *Body of State* is no exception. A veteran of stage and screen in Italy, Baliani has been involved in nearly all aspects of the broad spectrum spanning dramaturgy and theatrical presentation and all points in between. Of his many productions (some of which are listed below) *Body of State* and *Black Pinocchio* (2004) exemplify some of Baliani's inclinations. In both of these productions, Baliani approaches an historical event, social process, and cultural problem. Baliani's performances of *Body of State* give history a subjective face, body, and experience. As witness to the embodied and shared experience, audience members are drawn into reflection on the history of Italian politics in the First Republic (1946–1994), and, consequently, into contemplation of the motives that drove some Italians, largely of the generation just mentioned, to working outside of the pale of democracy and Parliament. This, in turn, leads to a consideration of the radical decision to enter into clandestine terrorism. Who are these terrorists? Are they monsters, radical political deviants whose experience cannot possibly tally with my own? Or might I know some of them from rallies I attended? Might I have dated a few, or gone to bed with others—or wanted to?[2] Baliani carefully measures the distance between his narrator and other young Italians, stripping away the demonization to humanize the terrorists, all the while holding them accountable for their actions.

Black Pinocchio, on the other hand, tells of a process opposite to that of *Body of State*. The performance, and the three-year-long process that brought it to the stage, concerns democratic inclusion, participation, and enfranchisement. From 2002 to 2004, Baliani worked with a group of orphans living in squalor in Nairobi's slum. After months of theater games and movement, the troupe—working in a group home in Nairobi—began working on their version of "Pinocchio." Months of preparation led to performances at the Bomas Theatre, the Godown, the AMREF Center, and the United Nations Mission in Nairobi (August 21–24, 2004). To be able to participate in the troupe's performances in Rome (September 2–3, 2004) and Palermo (September 8–9, 2004), the troupe's members needed passports for international travel. This was difficult for the orphaned boys, who did not know their family background. After some bureaucratic machinations, the boys secured passports legitimating their Kenyan citizenship. This broadly based, grassroots, from-the-bottom-up process of identification contrasts with the project of *Body of State*, in which historical memory is first channeled into an individual who then projects it back, writ large. This sort of civic-based theater that aims to provide public and political commentary aligns Baliani's work to Anna Deveare Smith's, Eve Ensler's, and Spaulding Gray's, to cite just several North American practitioners of a similar genre.

From the title of this narrative itself, *Body of State*, one sees Baliani's critical (and self-reflexive) position vis-à-vis the 1978 kidnapping and execution of Moro. The Italian reads *Corpo di Stato*; "corpo" means "body," but homophonically, with the switch of a single consonant, it recalls "co*l*po," meaning blow or following the French, coup, as in "coup d'état." A *colpo di stato*, or coup d'état, was indeed one of the aims of the BR, who, asserting Moro would be returned unharmed if imprisoned BR members were freed, held him in the "people's prison" in Rome, a tiny cell behind a false wall, where they "tried" him for crimes (symbolic as well as, in the BR's eyes, real) against the Italian public, found him guilty, and executed him. In fact, the BR's aim was a "*colpo al cuore dello stato*," or a blow to the heart of the State. But the homophonic relation between *corpo* and *colpo*, body and coup, is not merely a slip of the tongue.

In ways that are similar to the Bologna *Antigone* project (which is described below and on which Baliani reflects in the "diary" chapter), *Body of State* allows the author-narrator to elaborate the mourning of the as yet "unburied" body of Moro in political terms, reckoning with Moro's revenant, as the undead are known, and his effect on the devolution of the Italian Left in the years that followed the Moro Affair. Baliani re/collects the memories and sense of guilt of an entire generation—his own—which at the time of the abduction and assassination of Moro was confused and uncertain about which side to take. Like many young Italians involved in the "Movimento" (the "Movement," as the loose collective of Left-tending political cooperatives was called), Baliani felt sympathy for some of the terrorists' aims, but not their methods. This sympathy also produced overwhelming grief and guilt, not only for the loss of life but also for the way that the Moro Affair decimated the growth and sustainability of the Italian Left in the decades that followed the events.

As a translation, *Body of State* does not assume knowledge of Italian language, culture, and society. For this reason, the sections that follow address the context out of which Baliani's narrative emerged. The context starts by framing the historical and socio-political context in general terms before moving in the direction of a detailed picture. The history of Italy's government since the Second World War is thick with the names of multiple governments composed of multiple-party coalitions. Details, including names of political parties, names of individuals, dates, and translations of terms, are matched to the broad lines in an effort to portray the rich context of Baliani's narrative.[3]

Historical Context

Body of State brings into dialogue two historic moments: 1978, the year of Aldo Moro's kidnapping and assassination, and its commemoration twenty years later. Baliani does not collapse these two specific contexts indistinguishably. Rather, their separation is of some importance in understanding the work as a whole. We might say that the way Baliani brings these two historical points together works like the "fold" that Gilles Deleuze has described, wherein two discrete points on a continuum—either spatial or temporal—are brought together for comparison.[4] Like the folds of fabric, or in a fan, for example, the points of the historical continuum can be extended to their widest distance, like a measure of fabric pulled taut by outstretched arms. Such extension reveals the continuum in its entirety. Alternatively, should the fabric be folded, either by drawing the ends together or by pleating the fabric at some other place, the points can be drawn quickly together, bringing into proximity events that would otherwise be separated by historical time. Baliani enacts a spatial folding, for example, when he draws together for comparison events that occurred the same day but in the two discrete points of Via Caetani in Rome, where Moro's body was found, and the railroad tracks outside of Cinisi, not far from Palermo, in Sicily, where the dead body of political and anti-Mafia activist Peppino Impastato was found. The historical alternation in Baliani's monologue works similarly, between distinct moments in time between 1978 and 1998. In a similar fashion, and in the interests of understanding the effect of drawing them together, it is useful to understand the historical points in their "actual" historical context.

The kidnapping in 1978 of Aldo Moro by left-wing terrorists emerged from a social and historical context in Italy reaching back to the immediate postwar period, the very moment Calvino describes. The transition to democracy in Italy following the Second World War can be characterized generally as illustrating the worry that Italy would revert to its recent "black," or fascist, past or that it would slip into the "red," or communist, Eastern bloc. In postwar Italian politics, the Christian Democrats (DC) established an early and firm grip on a majority in parliament that lasted over thirty years, and was the hegemonic political presence for Italy's entire First Republic. Although the DC had brought into the fold of its coalition the Partito Socialista Italiano (PSI) in the 1960s, notably during Aldo Moro's first three governments (December 1963–June 1968), the Partito Comunista Italiano (PCI) had been excluded from every majority since 1948, since the third and last constitutional assembly before the First Republic.

Italy experienced a dual transition at the end of the Second World War: from the experience of fascism (1922–1943) and from the years of civil war between the fascist militia and the partisans. In the decades that followed this transition, the fear that Italy would turn "red" remained, fueling some of the opposition to the *compromesso storico*, the "historic compromise" that the moderate Enrico Berlinguer proposed, beginning in 1973. The PCI party secretary's aim was to join for the first time the Communist Party and the DC in a governing coalition. Sensing a stalemate in the democratic process of the Italian state, Berlinguer might have also sought to diminish the *strategia della tensione*, or the strategy of tension. This was a covert plan to keep political parties on the Left divided and unable to achieve a majority coalition. A large cast of players was interested in preventing a broad-based coalition of the Left, including the Italian Secret Services buttressed by the U.S. Central Intelligence Agency (CIA): Gladio, a stay-behind operation backed by the North Atlantic Treaty Organization (NATO), tasked with ensuring that the Communist Party—and by extension Soviet dominance—did not spread in Europe following the 1945 Yalta agreements. In addition to Gladio, Propaganda 2 (P2) also played a role in the strategy of tension. This was an undercover organization within an influential Masonic lodge stewarded by Licio Gelli that featured among its membership high ranking officials in the Italian government.

Opposing these reactionary forces in the background, players and movements in the political foreground suggested seemingly progressive developments. An example of this is found in the *Statuto dei Lavoratori*, or the Workers' Rights Bill, passed in May 1970. It guaranteed a minimum hourly wage, a forty-hour workweek, and other policies like, for example, the guaranteed right to 150 hours of educational benefits. A very obvious progressive move was the naming of Tina Anselmi in 1976 to the post of minister of labor, the first time a woman had been appointed to any cabinet position in government. Publicly, at least, Prime Minister Giulio Andreotti's third DC-led government (July 1976–March 1978) showed a relatively progressive position vis-à-vis the historic compromise inasmuch as he did not show open opposition to it. Moro was, in fact, on his way to the first parliamentary debate in Andreotti's fourth government, constituted on March 11, 1978, when he was kidnapped in Via Fani. En route to Montecitorio, Moro's motorcade was attacked, five members of his escort were killed, and he was abducted, all acts for which the BR took sole responsibility. This Via Fani attack represented the wished-for blow to the heart of the State.[5]

More than any other member of his political party, Aldo Moro was considered the prime mover of the official politics of the Christian Democrats. Moro graduated from the University of Bari in his native region of Puglia with a degree in jurisprudence in 1938 and his election to the Constituent Assembly in 1946 as a representative of the Christian Democrats set him on his path of career politician. Moro occupied various cabinet positions in the early years of the DC's hegemonic hold on Italian politics, including prime minister, minister of Grazia and Giustizia (Italy's Justice Department), of foreign affairs, and of education. In 1958 he joined a group of Christian Democrats, the so-called *dorotei*, who wished to move the party in a different direction from the ruling faction; after Moro was elected party secretary, his followers were known as *morotei*.

Aldo Moro served as the prime minister of DC-led governments five times: in three successive terms from December 1963 to June 1968 and for another two successive terms from November 1974 to July 1976. It was in this last two-term period that Moro helped foster the conditions in which the PCI might be brought into the ruling coalition in the historic compromise detailed above. In keeping with the movement between the foreground and the background of the political situation in Italy in the 1970s, Aldo Moro's open and avowed positions on a host of social topics and legislations could be why Pier Paolo Pasolini (1922–1975) found Moro to be "il meno implicato di tutti nelle cose orribili che sono state organizzate dal '69 ad oggi, nel tentativo, finora formalmente riuscito di conservare comunque il potere" [the least implicated of all in the horrible things that have been organized since 1969, in the attempt, so far successful, to preserve power no matter what].[6]

More than any other political party since the start of the First Republic in 1948, the DC dominated Italian politics. Buoyed by Vatican support within Italy, and, abroad, a network of nations and organizations ordained by the United States, the DC enjoyed primacy in majority coalitions in the First Republic. By the time of the Moro Affair in 1978, the DC had provided twelve prime ministers who helmed thirty-three DC-led governments until Giovanni Spadolini of the Partito Repubblicano Italiano (PRI) [Italian Republican Party] broke the uninterrupted Christian Democrat reign in June 1981.

If Italian politics appeared poised for transformation in the middle of the 1970s, it reflected the considerable changes taking place within Italian society. In 1970, the same year of the Workers' Rights Bill, a law was passed making divorce possible and, in May 1978, a law was passed guaranteeing Italian women the right to abortion. Debates concerning this law were also percolating alongside discussion of the historic compromise at the beginning of Andreotti's fourth term and the time of Moro's kidnapping. Following unprecedented growth until approximately 1960 in what is known as Italy's "economic miracle," by the mid-1970s, the Italian economy had grown sluggish. Thus, despite the educational reforms of the early 1960s, which had provided greater access to Italian universities to a wider constituency, few job opportunities awaited the 44 percent of matriculants who eventually finished their degrees.[7] A disaffected younger generation of students was joined by a workers' movement that increasingly questioned leadership and management of the labor unions. Radicalized university students and professors shared similar concerns, chief among which was a profound mistrust of those in entrenched positions of power.

The social activist movements of the 1970s, which Baliani brings to life with great detail in his narrative, sought to change the seat of power. For young Italian communists, the PCI was a great disappointment and the thought of the party entering into an accord with the Christian Democrats sounded a sort of death knell.[8] A historic compromise may have been afoot in the *palazzo* but it met with a remarkably uncompromising attitude of a radicalized swath of activists that embraced political violence as an effective means to an end.[9] With the ratcheting up of political violence in the 1970s, some members of the Left felt increasingly deprived of viable alternatives. As the Sicilian writer and member of Parliament representing the Radical Party, Leonardo Sciascia, wrote in *Lotta Continua* a year before the Moro kidnapping, he stood "neither with the Red Brigades nor with the Italian State."[10] As Baliani's narrative clarifies, this was the no-man's-land that many members of the Left found themselves in during Moro's fifty-five days of captivity.

As elsewhere throughout Europe and the Americas, Italy also experienced the social upheaval of the student and youth movements of the 1960s. The ways in which political violence—emanating from either the political Right or Left—was condoned and employed is a distinguishing feature of Italy's situation. The historiography of Italian terrorism has shown how problematic it was for the Italian polity to distinguish between terrorist actions authored by the Right or the Left. *Stragismo*, or the indiscriminate bombing like that in Piazza Fontana, about which we say more directly, was characteristic of political violence of the Right. More representative of left-wing political terrorism was the surgical strike against individuals in specific positions of power or public information.[11]

The explosion in the Banca Nazionale dell'Agricoltura in Milan's Piazza Fontana exemplifies the use of political violence as well as the response to it on the part of the Italian forces of law and order. On Friday, December 12, 1969, at 4:30 p.m., a bomb was detonated in the Banca Nazionale in this piazza in the heart of Milan, resulting in eighteen deaths and the wounding of eighty-six others.[12] Additionally, three bombs exploded in Rome the same day. Approximately four thousand "known" activists on the political Left were arrested throughout Italy that day and the next. On Monday, December 15, Giuseppe (Pino) Pinelli, an anarchist, was arrested by the Milan police and taken to headquarters for interrogation. Around midnight, Pinelli "fell" to his death from a window of the fourth floor office of Inspector Luigi Calabresi, head of the Piazza Fontana investigation. In late 1971, Milan's district attorney served Calabresi with an *avviso di garanzia*, or an intention to file criminal charges, for the murder of Pinelli.

The events of Piazza Fontana and the death of Giuseppe Pinelli under mysterious conditions set in motion a chain of events leading to the beginning of the years of lead. In October 1970, Calabresi filed a civil suit against *Lotta Continua*, the daily paper of the Movement, a loose coalition of leftist political organizations that Baliani describes in *Body of State*. The paper's assertions that Calabresi was the agent of and responsible for Pinelli's death led the officer to sue for defamation of character.[13] Leaving his Milan home on May 17, 1972, Calabresi was gunned down in the street. After numerous trials, three high-ranking members of Lotta Continua—Ovidio Bompressi, Adriano Sofri, and Giorgio Pietrostefani—were convicted and sentenced to life in prison. Doubts, especially concerning Sofri's role, emerged during the trials that led eventually to calls for the vacation of the convictions. Sofri has always maintained his innocence.

This was the Italian social and political context when, on March 16, 1978, Moro's guard was attacked and killed in a precisely orchestrated ambush in Via Fani, in which the former prime minister was kidnapped. Italian public reception of the abduction evolved over the nearly two months he was captive in the "People's Prison," a *covo*, or clandestine safe house used by the BR, somewhere in greater metropolitan Rome. The BR's plan had been to use Moro as leverage: the former prime minister would be released unharmed in exchange for incarcerated BR comrades. The number of the hostages to be exchanged fluctuated in correspondence with the BR's perceptions of the strength—or weakness—of their position. At the beginning of Moro's sequester they sought release of the nucleus of BR founding members, including Renato Curcio and Alberto Franceschini. By the end of Moro's detention, the BR probably would have been satisfied by the exchange of a single political prisoner for Moro's freedom. The terrorists' demands were made public by the nine communiqués sent during Moro's sequester, which were disseminated to the public by way of their publication in the media.[14] Moro also sent over ninety letters from the People's Prison to colleagues in his Christian Democrat Party, in other political parties, in other wings of government, and even, famously, to Pope Paul VI.[15]

Moro's letters became the object of dispute among ranking members of the DC. Ever prudent, Moro expressed to his colleagues his comprehension of the government's reluctance to negotiate with a terrorist organization. His understanding of the political dilemma notwithstanding, Moro endorsed the strategy of bargaining and exchanging of political prisoners. It was, he argued, in the interests of "Christian" charity for his position. Subjected to various authentication practices, the letters, the DC determined, had not been written by Moro himself but rather by his captors. As forgeries, the letters could not be considered seriously and could not genuinely characterize Moro's position concerning negotiation. In other words, the DC concluded, "The Moro who speaks from the People's Prison is not the Moro we knew."[16] To say that it would have been difficult to imitate Moro's florid prose style is an understatement. In an amazing display of philological pyrotechnics, Sciascia exposed the reasons why the DC disavowed authorship of the letters: it enabled the government to realize its *linea della fermezza*, or policy of non-negotiation, with the BR.[17] But the DC was not alone in insisting on *fermezza*. While Bettino Craxi (PSI) made attempts to construct some sort of network within which to negotiate with the terrorists, the Communist Party resolutely stood with the Christian Democrats in maintaining a non-negotiation policy. In one of his last letters, dated April 7, 1978, and addressed to his wife, Eleonora, Moro inveighs against his former colleagues in rhetoric that is nothing short of biblical. He predicts that, for their actions and decisions, "[i]l mio sangue ricadrà su di loro" [my blood will rain down on them].[18]

Despite a massive police blockade that had brought Rome to its knees, somehow Moro's body was transported from the People's Prison, located somewhere outside the city center (perhaps in Via Montalcini, though this has not been demonstrated), to the very heart of the capital on May 9, 1978. Moro's body, what Baliani terms his "body of state," was found in Via Caetani, midway between the seat of government since 1948, Montecitorio, and the seat of the Roman Empire, the Roman Forum, from which *Body of State* would be broadcast on public television on May 9, 1998.

Marco Baliani invites us to meditate on the location of Moro's cadaver and its ability to index the deep social and political contestation in Italy in 1978 and beyond. Moro's dead body is, like that of Polyneices in Sophocles's *Antigone*, unable to be buried. Unburied, it cannot be mourned.[19]

Body of State and the Theater of Narration

In *Body of State*, Baliani re/collects the memories of an entire generation that experienced great confusion and uncertainty during the Moro Affair about which side to take. Like many young Italians involved in the "Movimento," Baliani often supported the terrorists, but not without overwhelming grief and guilt.

When Baliani performed *Corpo di Stato* on public television in 1998, it did not yet have the stable shape it takes in this translation. The current version derives from the 2003 transcription of the original text, which Baliani conceived as something he calls an "oral flux." The process of creation, performance, and then scripted narrative is typical of Baliani's theater work, and may be fully understood only in the context of *teatro di narrazione*, or theater of narration, in which dramaturgy is seen as an act of creation that takes place directly on stage and in the context of its unfolding.

The theater of narration is a genre original to contemporary Italian theater and Baliani is acknowledged as one of its most representative practitioners.[20] This new type of performance rejects dramatic action in the conventional sense and predicates on the central role of the narrator—often the only character on stage—who is thus simultaneously subject, body, actor, and author. The narrator performs a subjective account of an historical fact or literary text, emphasizing the relationship between personal and collective experiences in the way Calvino intended by way of the artistic expression offered by performance. The audience, in Pasolini's words, listens instead of merely watching, and is not considered simply the addressee of the narrator's aesthetic and political message. Rather, the audience member is also identified with a wider community: spectators share the narrator's experience, history, and civic responsibility.[21]

As Baliani emphasizes,

> Il narratore non è un interprete e, come diceva Pasolini, nemmeno l'attore è un interprete, ma un uomo di cultura; e io sono pienamente d'accordo col fatto che attore e narratore abbiano compiti culturali e non rappresentativi.[22]

> [The narrator is not an interpreter and, as Pasolini said, neither is the actor. Rather, he is a man of culture. I fully agree that actor and narrator have cultural tasks, not those of representing reality.]

With the term "representing," Baliani points to the established theatrical tradition, in which both the author and the actor attempt to render the reality objectively, with the help of a meticulous mise-en-scène and a realistic acting. On the contrary, Baliani claims that the narrator and the actor have an important role in society's cultural and intellectual life; therefore, he is seeking nontraditional ways to interpret the reality, and, at the same time, to involve the audience in the discussion.

The theater of narration originates from this form of research. It developed in the 1990s within the framework of a well-established national tradition that was the result of the militant, 1970s-era activities of Dario Fo.[23] In the theater of narration, Fo's conception of theater as an instrument of political activism and as a performative recollection of popular memories merged with Pasolini's *teatro di parola*, or theater of the word, and with international theatrical experiences, such as Jerzy Grotowski's "poor" and Eugenio Barba's intercultural theater. Grotowski, and, after him, his pupil Barba, is the creator of "poor theater," which eliminates all nonessential elements—that is, costumes, sound effects, makeup, sets, lighting, and strictly designed playing area—in an effort to redefine the relationship between cast and audience.[24] In 1986 Barba opened the Workcenter in Pontedera, Italy, where his ideas about theater are still explored.

In his collection of theoretical reflections on storytelling and theater, Baliani claims the paternity of the theater of narration, dating it to *Kohlhaas*, his first solo actor performance from 1989 staging the story of a man, the Kohlhaas of the title, oppressed by a king's power and who decides to resist it. Adapted from Heinrich von Kleist's eponymous novella, *Kohlhaas* is now a renowned work in the repertory of the theater of narration. The narrative unfolds while the lone actor-narrator sits before the audience on a chair, a position he maintains for the duration of the performance:

Ventuno anni fa ho raccontato per la prima volta *Kohlhaas*. Seduto su una sedia per un'ora e mezza sperimentavo un teatro di pura narrazione. Da allora si chiamò così, teatro di narrazione, per tutti quelli, e furono e sono tanti, che seguirono il mio esempio, provando ciascuno in forme e contenuti diversi a ridurre lo spazio scenico ad un corpo narrante.[25]

[I told the story of *Kohlhaas* for the first time twenty-one years ago. Sitting on a chair for an hour and a half I experimented with a theater of pure narrative form. Ever since, it has taken this name, theater of narration, for all those playwrights and actors who, following my example, try to reduce the stage to one narrative body, in different forms and contents.]

Other practitioners who "followed his example" are the playwright-actors Ascanio Celestini, Laura Curino, Moni Ovadia, and Marco Paolini. Their works differ in content and style, but resemble Baliani's in terms of political engagement, focus on Italy's national past and society, and, especially, their form of storytelling. These authors were all broadcast on the public television in the late 1990s and, unexpectedly, received a great deal of attention from critics and the general theater-going public.[26] Since then, Ascanio Celestini has authored a number of monologues on World War II and the Resistance in which narration unfolds as a recollection of domestic, understated voices, like, for example, a mother, a grandmother, a father, or a child talking at the dinner table. Laura Curino's most famous piece, *Olivetti*, is based on the Olivetti family, founders of the Olivetti enterprise of typewriters, printers, and business machines. In this piece, she narrates the life of workers and employers in the Olivetti factory (in Turin) employing a mix of nostalgia and political reckoning. Marco Paolini is best known for *Il racconto del Vajont* [*The Story of Vajont*], a documentary-like narration of the 1963 Vajont Dam disaster. Bulgarian born Moni Ovadia is more of an outsider. Two of his projects, *Oylem Goylem* and *Dybbuk*, both feature the use of Yiddish as well as references to Jewish humor and music to convey the sense of alienation of the Jewish community in Italy and elsewhere.

Marco Baliani has explored the potential of the theater of narration in a number of ways, using his and his actors' bodies as the bearers of existential and political messages. Some of his narrative pieces revolve around the most controversial events of Italy's national past. In addition to *Body of State* on the Moro murder case, Baliani authored, for instance, *Antigone delle città* [*Antigone of the Cities*], a commemoration of the dead of the 1980 right-wing terrorist massacre at the Bologna train station. Baliani comments on this in the "diary" included in this volume. *Antigone* is truly a collective endeavor, with one hundred actors scattered around the city reciting poems and declaiming readings, while the citizens of Bologna participated, offering food and transportation to actors and crew.

Baliani links the theater of narration to the Western theatrical tradition, arguing that theater has always used "La pura narrazione, con racconti che si insinuavano sulla scena del dramma e del dialogo, così da permettere visioni di spazi e tempi altrimenti impossibili da rappresentare" [pure narration, with stories that were interspersed throughout the dramatic action and dialogue to allow the vision of spaces and times otherwise impossible to represent].[27] In other words, Baliani's actor-narrator plays the role of the messenger in Greek theater, whose entrance fills in the gaps with information about events that are remote in space or time. Interested in the "new points of view on the ongoing drama, discoveries, recognitions, new conflicts" that the narrator generated in classical theater, Baliani claims to have brought this role to its extreme:

> Il ruolo del narratore e della narrazione è dunque ben conosciuto da sempre. Io non ho fatto altro che prolungare all'estremo quel ruolo, facendo precipitare l'intero dramma dentro un'unica voce e un unico corpo. È stato un atto di estremismo sperimentale.[28]

> [The role of the narrator and of the narration has been well known from its very beginnings. I did nothing else but stretch that role to its extreme, condensing the entire drama into only one voice and one body. It was an act of experimental extremism.]

This particular aspect of Baliani's research is what makes his work unique in the panorama of the theater of narration. In fact, Baliani's narratives do not focus on the message conveyed by the narrator, but on his emotions that are evoked in performance. In Baliani's words:

> C'è un particolare flusso che può catturarti durante un racconto, se riesci a farlo esistere e ti ci lasci andare improvvisamente la storia pur tante volte ripetuta rivela grumi di sensazioni fisiche e sensoriali mai sperimentate prima. Quel *flusso* è la stella polare della mia ricerca, il mio allenamento spirituale all'arte del racconto.[29]

> [There is a particular flow that can capture you during a storytelling, if you can allow it to exist and let yourself go with it, all of a sudden the story, although repeated many times, reveals traces of physical and sensorial perceptions that you have never experienced before. That *flow* is the polestar of my research, my spiritual training in the art of storytelling.]

Memory has a particularly strong role in the act of storytelling: it helps the audience fill the gaps in their knowledge of the past and to draw further kinds of connections. Baliani calls this process "imaginative memory":

> Si mette in moto una speciale forma narrante della memoria, una memoria immaginativa che crea nel flusso del racconto continui nuovi tasselli e congiunzioni.[30]

> [A special narrative form of memory is activated, an imaginative memory that creates ongoing, new pieces of the mosaic and new combinations in the flow of the storytelling.]

The flow of orality is instrumental to the work of memory as Baliani conceives it. His goal is the same as Calvino's mentioned above: to remember collectively the "small stories" of the recent past—namely, the "microhistory, the work of the 'Annales'" that macrohistory has not recorded.[31] In this framework, the narration of *Body of State* aims to fill one of the "holes" in the collective memory that expands "from WWI up to the Red Brigades."[32]

Baliani's oral narratives link to experiences in Italy's national past that are, at once, historically controversial and personally intense. His attention to microhistory does not produce any sense of what is apparently casual, the typical everyday chatter that characterizes, for example, the theater practice of Ascanio Celestini, mentioned above as one of the protagonists of narrative theater. Baliani's narrative flow does not aim to chronicle the past nor to faithfully re-create it. On the contrary, it is a way for Baliani to review that past in search of points of conjunction that can help the actor and his audience imbue their faulty memories and personal anecdotes with both form and meaning. Indeed, Baliani is convinced that remembering and recounting serve our human need to recreate the "esperienza originale" [original experience] and to locate its "forma mitica" [mythical form].[33] To describe his idea of the relationships between narration, memory, and past, he borrows an image from Karen Blixen's parable of the stork in *Out of Africa*—that is, the idea of a trace on the sand:

> È come se, nel tentativo di riannodare il proprio passato, si cercasse a tutti i costi un filo che leghi gli episodi, che li trattenga in un ordito, ma questo filo è come un segno tracciato sulla sabbia del mare, sembra solido e deciso finché una piccola onda ne smangia un contorno, ne interrompe l'andamento, lasciando di colpo delle zone vuote nel tracciato. Colui che rammemora è appeso al filo di questo effimero percorso. Ad ogni ostacolo, ad ogni interruzione di linearità, dovrà intervenire ridisegnando segni che prima non

c'erano. . . . E comunque alla fine qualcosa sarà rimasto, aneddoti, episodi, accadimenti, che entreranno a far parte di una nostra personalissima mitologia.[34]

[It is as if in the attempt to re-craft one's past, one were at all costs looking for a thread that linked the episodes, that kept them in order. But this thread is like a sign traced in the sand at the seashore; it seems solid and defined until a small wave swallows one side, interrupting its path and leaving gaps in the trace. Whoever remembers hangs from the thread of this ephemeral path. Whenever an obstacle appears, whenever the linearity is interrupted, he will have to intervene, re-designing signs that were never there . . . and yet, in the end, something has always stayed behind: anecdotes, episodes, events that will become part of a very personal mythology.]

Baliani's "personal mythology" is evoked in *Body of State* on various levels of the text and is explicitly discussed in the extensive paratext surrounding the written version of the narrative. In these parts, Baliani offers considerable information about his preparatory work, and provides details regarding literary, political, and historical themes, the dramaturgic conception and scope of the text, and the connotations of the title. Along with standard paratextual elements, this volume includes a "diario," or "diary," a sort of meta-theatrical journal published in appendix to the actual narrative; a considerable number of documentary photos; and some pictures taken during the 1998 performance.[35] As Baliani emphasizes in his "diary," the dramaturgical catalyst of the conflict performed in *Body of State* is Moro's body. In Baliani's words, its cumbersome physicality as a "corpo immolato/destinato" [immolated/fated body] is the "asse calamitante" [magnetic axis] of his storytelling.[36]

In the "diary," Baliani explains how his theatrical research on *Antigone delle città*, the commemorative work on the Bologna massacre, led him to identify the mythical and archetypical references that, in his view, lie at the heart of the Moro murder case. These references evoke historical images of guilt, associating the body of Moro with the "carnaio" [carnage] of the Holocaust and claiming the dramatic conflict of Sophocles's *Antigone*. Speculating on the multiple meanings of the title, Baliani mentions "proprio quella scena antica, Antigone e il corpo insepolto del fratello" [precisely that ancient scene, Antigone and the unburied body of her brother].

In *Body of State*, these mythical images are not mentioned explicitly. Baliani's theater works on a dual level of representation, both emotional and intellectual. The narrative constantly swings between a Brechtian mode, in which the actor detaches himself from the events and raises the audience's awareness of it, and embodied interpretation, when the actor invokes the emotional participation of the public in his recounting. In this way, as Baliani's narrative unfolds, it alternates between objective and subjective remembering. The audience's reaction is concurrently one of stupor, intimacy, and detachment.

> Si passa da un'emotività partecipe e intensa ad una distanza improvvisamente fredda, dove è richiesta una lucidità del pensiero, per poi essere di nuovo colpiti da un soprassalto di stupore. Intimità e distanza si intrecciano, empatia e straniamento avvengono in contemporanea, lo spettatore vede me che racconto ma al tempo stesso percepisce l'immaginario che gli sto evocando. Ciò che gli appare sulla scena, il mio corpo seduto che racconta, sembra del tutto oggettivo eppure al contempo su un piano soggettivo sta vivendo intensamente un'altra realtà. Nella narrazione il concatenarsi degli eventi non è una questione di intelligibilità, le cose accadono senza dover sempre ricorrere ad una spiegazione di tipo causale, agiscono attraverso le metafore fisiche che il corpo mette in scena.[37]

> [You move from one intense participatory emotion to, suddenly, a cold distance in which clarity of thought is required and then you give a gasp of shocked amazement. Intimacy and distance are linked, empathy and alienation concurrently overlap. The spectator sees me narrating but, at the same time, perceives the imaginary I am evoking. What appears on stage—my seated body narrating—seems completely objective and yet, at the same time, on a subjective plane, is experiencing intensely another reality. In the narration, the sequencing of events is not a matter of intelligibility: things sometimes happen without causal explanations, they act by way of physical metaphors that the body puts into the scene.]

This passage exemplifies Baliani's ideas on narrative theater in general, and particularly on *Kohlhaas*. Yet it is also useful for *Body of State*. The uniqueness of *Body of State* consists in the fact that the narrator's voice coincides not only with that of the author but—unusually in Baliani's theater—also with that of the narrated self. This powerful combination unifies fragments of memory and invokes images and myths of an entire generation as they decay. In this sense, *Body of State* is considerably more political than Baliani's other works, for the "risveglio" [reawakening] of the audience's remembering takes place in the form of reasoning, at a time of full awareness.[38] In other words, because the narrative naturally intertwines with the actor's persona in the historical context, *Body of State* makes the political circumstances explicit. This is not to say that this is the only instance of political production in Baliani's corpus. Indeed, by focusing on the struggle between the individual and power *tout court*, Baliani's theater is always political in a broader sense. What is profoundly political is the exhortation of the audience to meditate on this particular conflict. The fact that this "reawakening" happens on the personal level of the audience member, accords with the slogan of Baliani's generation that the "personal is political." As Baliani notes,

> Fin dalle prime azioni del racconto devo riuscire a mettere in crisi credenze e aspettative, ma non in maniera traumatica, devo fare in modo che lo spiazzamento percettivo a cui sottopongo lo spettatore avvenga gradualmente, e che soprattutto ne sia consapevole, è questo il senso politico del mio raccontare, voglio che il risveglio avvenga anche coscientemente.[39]

> [From the story's beginning, I must interrogate [the audience's] beliefs and expectations, but not traumatically. I must achieve this in such a way that the disorientation of perception to which I subject the spectator comes about gradually and that above all she or he does this consciously. This is the political fact of my story-telling. I want the reawakening to come about consciously.]

The Current Work

Marco Baliani's acclaimed dramatic narrative *Body of State* is offered here in a comprehensive study. In his preface Ron Jenkins, performance studies scholar and translator of Dario Fo, focuses on the concept of montage as it relates to *Body of State*, with particular reference to the performances that took place in North America in the spring of 2009. Following the annotated translation is Baliani's "diary." This prose piece collects the actor-writer's thoughts on the preparation of *Body of State* in 1998 and, as we mentioned above, his thoughts on the performance of *Antigone delle città* in 1991 in Bologna. Reflecting on the rehearsals and public performances commemorating the victims of the massacre at the Bologna train station in 1980 perpetrated by the right-wing terrorists, Baliani uses Sophocles's tragedy as a lens through which to see the difficult "burial" of Moro.

Following these translations is an interview with Baliani in New York City in April 2009 as the *Body of State* tour drew to a close after engagements at Indiana University, Wesleyan University, Dickinson College, Yale University, Northwestern University, and Middlebury College, as well as the Italian Cultural Institutes of Washington, D.C., and Chicago. The appendix that appears at the end of the book collects reviews from spectators of the various performances and includes impressions from colleagues—and, uniquely, students—from a wide variety of disciplines. The text's concluding chapter is Marco Baliani's and director Maria Maglietta's "afterword," in which they narrate their emotional and intellectual discovery of the academic and urban contexts experienced in the 2009 North American tour.

Body of State has resources for scholars and teachers alike, and the text is intended for an audience interested in both uses. This project represents an unusual collaboration between the translators, who work at three different universities, and still other colleagues at the institutions where *Body of State* was performed. We are grateful to Baliani for this other story that his theater has generated.

Marco Baliani: Background, Theater, Film

Marco Baliani has written, directed, and acted in a number of theatrical works. His first production, in 1978, was the play for children *Storia di Petrosinella* (1978), of which he provides a description in *Body of State*. With Maria Maglietta and the group of "Ruotalibera Teatro," he then staged *Popout* (1979), *Souperman* (1982), *Rosa e Celeste* (1983), *Orphy 2013* (1984), *Oz* (1986), *Tisiù* (1988), *Storie* (1988), *Jeanne d'Arc* (1989), and *Saturnus* (1989). The adaptation from Heinrich von Kleist's novella, *Kohlhaas* (1989), that he performed on a bare stage, sitting on a chair for one hour and a half, marked his passage to a "pure" theater of narration and is today a classic of the genre.

Since *Kolhaas*, Baliani has shown interest in social, political, and literary themes. A recurrent topic of his theater is the psychological and ethical tensions that arise when the search for justice clashes with power or social injustice. He has explored such tensions in various contexts—for instance, in *Gioventù senza Dio* (1997), adapted from Ödön Von Horvàt, which depicts the coming to power of Nazism; *La crociata dei fanciulli: Ballata per canto e corpi* (1999), adapted from Marcel Schwob's and Jerzy Andrzejewski's works, which dramatizes the children's crusade of 1212; and *Francesco a testa in giù* (2000) and *La seconda vita di Francesco d'Assisi* (2000), which focus on Francis of Assisi's rebellion against poverty and violence.

Still engaged with the issues raised by political and social conflicts, Baliani created and directed several works on the collective memory of the historical past troubled by war or terrorism: *Corvi di luna* (1989), *D'acqua la luna* (1990), *La buona novella* (1990), *Antigone delle città (2 agosto 1991)*, *Parole* (1991), *Antigoni della terra (2 agosto 1992)*, *Memoria del fuoco* (1992), *Memorie del gelso: Intorno ai racconti e alla memoria storica della città di Alessandria* (1992), *Frollo* (1993), *Piccoli angeli* (1993), *Come gocce di una fiumana* (1994), and *Anni di vento* (1995). Finally, *Di scomode parole* (2007) is a political and human dialogue about the ideas of socialism, sacrifice, betrayal, and martyrdom through the figure of the Italian patriot Cesare Battisti. Maria Maglietta coauthored and codirected many of these works. Some of them were indeed the result of the collective efforts of a number of actors and other collaborators, who recited archival documents from World War I and the Resistance or contemporary poets' works (in the two *Antigones*, for instance). It will be now clear how *Body of State: The Moro Affair, A Nation Divided* (1998) is at the center of Baliani's theatrical experience inasmuch as it fits both in this context as a commemorative work and in the area of interest highlighted above as a political work.

A substantial corpus of Baliani's and Maglietta's plays reflects the current debate on immigration and multiculturalism. In the framework of the project "I Porti del Mediterraneo," or the Ports of the Mediterranean, they conceived with an international group *Migranti* (1996), *Giufà* (1997), *Sguardi incrociati* (1998), *Pensare il pensiero degli altri* (1999), and *Sacrificë* (2000). For several years, in addition, Baliani has volunteered with AMREF, an international organization that supports the poor countries of Africa. With AMREF, he carried out the projects *Black Pinocchio*, outlined above, and *L'amore buono, una ballata ai tempi dell'AIDS* (2006).

Baliani has also adapted a number of classic literary works, such as *E d'accanto mi passano femmine* (2000) from Cesare Pavese; *Bertoldo* (2001) from Giulio Cesare Croce; *Lear* (1994) from Shakespeare; *Peer Gynt* (1994) from Ibsen; *Prima che il gallo canti* (1994) from Cesare Pavese; *Tracce* (1996) from Ernst Bloch; *Metamorphosen* (1998) from Ovid; *Sole nero* (1998) from Gina Negrini; *Le serve* (2002) from Jean Genet; *Lo straniero* (2003) from Albert Camus; and *La pelle* (2008) from Curzio Malaparte. In 2007, he worked on *La notte delle lucciole*, an original adaptation of Pasolini's and Sciascia's reflections on the disappearance of the fireflies. In 2010, Baliani staged *Piazza d'Italia*, from Antonio Tabucchi's novel, which discusses the notion of cultural identity within the framework of the one hundred fiftieth anniversary of the unification of Italy. Finally, Baliani created and directed *La cena in Emmaus* (2005), a play that intertwines the work of theater with that of painting through the figure of Caravaggio.

Baliani regularly works as an actor in plays written and directed by other authors. He acted in Mario Martone's adaptation of Aeschylus's *I sette contro Tebe* (1996), Massimo Luconi's play from Sandro Veronesi's novel *No man's land* (2003), and Giovanni Testori's interpretation of Manzoni's *The Betrothed* titled *La monaca di Monza* (2004), directed by Sandro Veronesi.

Marco Baliani played leading and secondary roles in several feature films: *Teatri di guerra* (1998) by Mario Martone; *Domani* (2001) by Francesca Archibugi; *Il più bel giorno della mia vita* (2002) by Cristina Comencini; *Il ronzio delle mosche* (2003) by Dario D'Ambrosi; *Il silenzio dell'allodola* (2005) by David Ballerini; *Viaggio segreto* (2006) by Roberto Andò; *In memoria di me* (2007) by Saverio Costanzo; *La ragazza del lago* (2007) by Andrea Molaioli; and *Il passato è una terra straniera* (2008) by Daniele Vicari.[40]

Notes

1. Italo Calvino, *The Path to the Spiders' Nest*, translated by A. Colquhoun, revised by Martin McLaughlin (New York: HarperCollins, 2000), 144.

2. For a reading of the social and cultural demonization of terrorists, see Marie Orton, "De-monstering the Myth of the Terrorist Woman: Faranda, Braghetti, and Mambro," *Romance Languages Annual* 16 (1998): 281–96; and Ruth Glynn, "Terrorism, a Female Malady," in *Terrorism, Italian Style: Representations of Political Violence in Contemporary Italian Cinema*, edited by Ruth Glynn, Giancarlo Lombardi, and Alan O'Leary (London: IGRS Books, forthcoming).

3. Annotations for *Body of State* include detailed notes explaining Baliani's references to various political entities.

4. See Gilles Deleuze, *The Fold, Liebniz, and the Baroque*, foreword and translation by Tom Conley (Minneapolis: University of Minnesota Press, 1992), 3–27.

5. See Robin Wagner-Pacifici, *The Moro Morality Play: Terrorism as Social Drama* (Chicago: University of Chicago Press, 1986); and Ellen Nerenberg, "To Strike at the Heart of State and Family: Gianni Amelio's *Colpire al Cuore*," in *Terrorism, Italian Style: Representations of Political Violence in Contemporary Italian Cinema*, edited by Ruth Glynn, Giancarlo Lombardi, and Alan O'Leary (London: IGRS Books, forthcoming).

6. Pier Paolo Pasolini, *L'articolo delle lucciole* (Milan: Mondadori, 1999), 410.

7. Aurelio Lepre, *Storia della Prima Repubblica: L'Italia dal 1944 al 1992* (Bologna: Il Mulino, 1993), 223.

8. Baliani prefers narrative to monologue. This is elaborated in greater detail below. See also the interview later in this volume.

9. Pier Paolo Pasolini first introduced the architectural metaphor of *Palazzo* [Palace] as the place of hegemony in his newspaper article "Fuori dal Palazzo" [Outside the Palace], published in *Lettere Luterane* (Turin: Einaudi, 1976), 92–97.

10. "Elogio della viltà," *Lotta Continua*, June 13, 1977, 1, cited in Richard Drake, "The Aldo Moro Murder Case in Retrospect," *Journal of Cold War Studies* 8:2 (2006): 115.

11. Other classic examples of *stragismo* include the bombing of the Italicus train (1974), the bombing of Piazza della Loggia in Brescia (1974), and the bombing of the Bologna train station in 1980. Examples of the sort of precise and surgical actions perpetrated by the Left included the kidnapping of Siemens executive Idalgo Macchiarini (1972), the magistrate Mario Sossi (1972), and U.S. General James Dozier (1981), among others. In their study, Pier Paolo Antonello and Alan O'Leary define left-wing political terrorism as guerrilla actions. See their *Imagining Terrorism: The Rhetoric and Representation of Political Violence in Italy, 1969–2006* (London: Legenda, 2009).

12. Giorgio Boatti, *Piazza Fontana. 12 dicembre 1969: Il giorno dell'innocenza perduta* (Turin: Einaudi, 1999), 15–16.

13. Two months later, in December 1970, Dario Fo debuted his acclaimed play based on the events, *The Accidental Death of an Anarchist*. Dario Fo, *Accidental Death of an Anarchist*, adapted by Richard Nelson, based on a literal translation by Suzanne Cowan; with editing by Ron Jenkins and Joel Schechter (New York: Samuel French, 1987).

14. http://www.fondazioneitaliani.it/index.php/en/Brigate-Rosse.-Comunicati
-durante-il-sequestro-Moro.html, accessed April 20, 2010.

15. Miguel Gotor estimates that Moro wrote ninety-seven texts from prison. The exact number is complicated because some letters were thought to have been written and delivered and yet the recipients did not circulate them. See Miguel Gotor, *Aldo Moro, lettere dalla prigionia* (Turin: Einaudi, 2008).

16. Leonardo Sciascia, *The Moro Affair*, translated by Sacha Rabinovitch (Manchester, UK: Carcanet, 1987), 56.

17. By endowing the title of his essay with "Affair," Sciascia invokes the case of the Dreyfus Affair, and the accusation of treason of Alfred Dreyfus, a Jewish captain in the French military at the end of the nineteenth century. The case was notorious for its trumped-up accusations, eliciting an incendiary letter from French author Emile Zola, published in January 1898 in the newspaper *L'Aurore*, titled "J'accuse!" See Giuseppina Mecchia, "Moro's Body between Enlightenment and Postmodernism: Terror, Murder and Meaning in Jean Baudrillard and Leonardo Sciascia," *Re-membering Moro: the Cultural Legacy of the Kidnapping and Death of Aldo Moro* (Oxford: Legenda, forthcoming).

18. See also Ellen Nerenberg, "Doxa, Orthodox, Heterodox, Paradox, Oxymoron: Aldo Moro's *Lettere dalla prigione del popolo*," in *Re-membering Moro*.

19. For an analysis of the idea of mourning in *Body of State* and the associations with *Antigone*, see Nicoletta Marini-Maio, "Unbury That Body: The Tragic Palinode of a Generation in Marco Baliani's *Corpo di Stato*," in *Re-membering Moro*.

20. Due to the novelty of the *teatro di narrazione*, there is no agreement yet about its categorization as a genre, a trend, or a style. Simone Soriani, for example, defines it a "quasi-genere" [almost-genre]. See "Dario Fo, il teatro di narrazione, la nuova 'performance' epica: Per una genealogia d'un 'quasi-genere,'" *Forum Italicum* 39:2 (Fall 2005): 620–48. In fact, the number of the productions, their specific features, and their civic and their collective nature make *teatro di narrazione* unique in the panorama of Italian contemporary theater, making the case for its definition as a new genre.

21. See Pier Paolo Pasolini, "Manifesto," *Nuovi argomenti* 9 (1968): 7.

22. See Marco Baliani, "Esperienza—tempo—verità: un seminario sulla narrazione," in *La bottega dei narratori: Storie, laboratori e metodi di: Marco Baliani, Ascanio Celestini, Laura Curino, Marco Paolini, Gabriele Vacis*, edited by Gerardo Guccini (Rome: Dino Audino Editore, 2005), 63. Baliani is here again making reference to Pasolini's "Manifesto."

23. Soriani, in "Dario Fo, il teatro di narrazione" (see note 20), strongly emphasizes the relationship between Fo and the theater of narration.

24. With regard to Pasolini's notion of *teatro di parola*, see Pier Paolo Pasolini, "Manifesto," in *Nuovi argomenti* 9 (1968): 6–22, and William Van Watson, *Pier Paolo Pasolini and the Theater of the Word* (Ann Arbor: UMI Research Press, 1989). Fo's career as a playwright and actor has been characterized by the use of theater as an active instrument of political struggle. Because of his problematic relationship with the *teatri stabili* and with the Italian public TV channel, for more than thirty years Fo and his wife Franca Rame held their performances in factories, universities, and public squares. For a systematic elaboration of Fo's thought on the politics and aesthetics of theater, see Dario Fo, *Manuale minimo dell'attore* (Turin: Einaudi, 1997).

25. Marco Baliani, *Ho cavalcato in groppa ad una sedia* (Pisa: Titivillus, 2010), 9 [our translation].

26. The numerous and uninterrupted theatrical replicas of Baliani's, Celestini's, Curino's, and Paolini's works in the *teatri stabili* of the most important Italian cities are a clear sign of the extraordinarily positive reception of the *teatro di narrazione* in Italy. In addition, the theatrical series broadcast on television in 1997 and 1998 was an unexpected success: Paolini's *Vajont*, for instance, captured a surprising share of 15.78 percent, with more than three million spectators. Cultural television programs usually have a very limited audience and theatrical performances on TV are considered minor productions, "roba adatta al massimo alla seconda serata . . . o magari ai quattro gatti e ai videoregistratori di *Fuori orario*" [stuff good at best for a second broadcast or maybe for the few spectators and the video recorders of *Fuori orario*]. Oliviero Ponte di Pino, "Le eccezioni e le regole: Sei spettacoli teatrali su Raidue," in *Olivieropdp per la cultura del teatro e dello spettacolo dal vivo*, http://www.trax.it/olivieropdp/teatrotv.htm, accessed April 30, 2010.

27. Marco Baliani, *Ho cavalcato*, 9.

28. Ibid., 40.

29. Ibid.

30. Ibid., 48.

31. Oliviero Ponte di Pino (ed.), "Il racconto. Una conversazione con Marco Baliani," in Marco Baliani and Remo Rostagno, *Kohlhaas* (Perugia: Futura, 2001), 22–23. On the notions of "microhistory" and "macrohistory," see Carlo Ginzburg, *The Cheese and the Worms: The Cosmos of a Sixteenth Century Miller* (Baltimore: Johns Hopkins University Press, 1980). Those involved in *Les Annales* were a group of largely French historians interested in recovering the rhythms of historical daily life as opposed to history's grand narratives. The historians of *Les Annales* have focused on structures, long duration, and the flow of development or growth. These are seen in contrast with an appreciation of the "grand narratives" and the roles played in historical change by battles, changing governments, and facts concerning kings and important political men. For a discussion of the notion of event as a problem, see Lucien Le Febvre, *Le problème de l'incroyance au XVI siècle* (Lucien, Paris: Albin Michel, 1947), and Marc Bloch, *Apologie pour l'histoire, ou, Métier d'historie* (Paris: A. Colin, 1993).

32. Marco Baliani, *Ho cavalcato*, 22.

33. Ibid., 48.

34. Ibid. Interestingly, Adriana Cavarero as well uses the same apologue to describe her idea of narration in *Tu che mi guardi, tu che mi racconti* [*Relating Narratives: Storytelling and Selfhood*] (Milan: Feltrinelli, 1997), 8–9. Franco Nasi elaborates on these connections in the appendix of this volume.

35. Marco Baliani, "Diario," in *Corpo di Stato*, 75–76.

36. Ibid., 85.

37. Marco Baliani, *Ho calvalcato*, 29–30.

38. For an illustration of the notion of "reawakening," see Peter Brook, *The Shifting Point* (New York: Harper & Row, 1987).

39. Marco Baliani, *Ho cavalcato*, 40–41.

40. Information on Marco Baliani's works and professional career is available on his official website: http://www.marcobaliani.it/ (accessed May 16, 2010).

CHAPTER 2

Body of State: The Moro Affair, a Nation Divided

MARCO BALIANI

Translated by Nicoletta Marini-Maio, Ellen Nerenberg, and Thomas Simpson

Valle Giulia, University of Rome, School of Architecture, Rome, 1973

The School of Architecture has been occupied for some months now. Outside, the windows are plastered with banners, there's graffiti all over the walls. The entryway is guarded by comrades assigned to the *servizio d'ordine*, working in shifts.[1]

We've hidden our helmets and tire irons, out of sight but close at hand.

On the top floor, the windows that open out onto the embankment leading up to Viale Bruno Buozzi are always unlocked, so we can flee in case the police decide to retake the building.

Students are coming and going all the time, running all the courses themselves. We've got building sciences, structural design, math. In the project planning classrooms on the third floor, someone has written a slogan on the wall: "Let's Take Back the City."

Study commissions have been formed: one is researching shady power relations between university fat cats and urban planners, another drafts reports for the squatters' committees in the occupied houses in the outlying neighborhoods.[2]

There are assemblies all the time in the main auditorium. Different student leaders of the extra-parliamentary groups take turns talking. They're all represented in the Architecture Political Committee, from Avanguardia Operaia to Manifesto to Lotta Continua to Potere Operaio, but their political positions diverge widely.[3]

After a few months of occupation fatigue sets in, attendance at the assemblies starts to drop off, lots of sleeping bags in the rooms on the top floor remain empty at night.

23

Starting some weeks ago, the most committed students in the occupation formed a sort of side group that I'm part of, too. Many play instruments. To pass the time, we organize little musical happenings. Dario Fo comes to visit and talks about the craft of acting. Using the abandoned classrooms, we make up little sketches mixing visual arts and performance, always with lots of music. We write up a statement titled *From Woodstock to Mirafiori* and hand it out.[4]

I find myself inventing characters, making up stories and plots, reading theater for the first time. We give birth to a sort of theatrical-musical improvisation based on a fable: *The King Is Naked*. Theater that's raw, simple, deeply political.

We decide to present the show in the main auditorium. Word goes out and at showtime the hall is packed with more people than we've seen in a long time.

The crowd applauds throughout the show, there's lots of enthusiasm.

At the end all the actors and musicians line up, about thirty of us, and we all salute the audience by singing *Bandiera rossa* with raised fists, but we twist the classic communist anthem with a blues rhythm and do a little dance number, like a chorus line in a musical.[5]

We notice, however, that only some of the audience laughs along with us.

A few days go by, then me and some other people in the theater group get summoned before the Political Committee. As soon as we enter the meeting room, we can tell the atmosphere is bad; angry, dark expressions on faces. They attack us right off; we try to defend ourselves but it's useless, we're face to face with a solid wall.

Finally, at the end, one of the comrades from Potere Operaio, an outsider, points his finger at us and then to the door and shouts, "Get out! Get out! These people are not comrades! They're actors, nothing but actors!"[6]

I'd been branded. That's how I started doing theater.

May 9, 1978, Via Montalcini, Rome. Dawn. Aldo Moro

They fired machine guns, a burst as he stood there in pajamas and undershirt looking like he'd just woken up, like some old Roman retiree.

They woke him up and took him down to the garage. What did they tell him that morning? That they were going to free him? That they'd reached an agreement? Or did they just tell him to follow them, nothing else?

Did Aldo Moro know it was the end? He must have seen his jailers' real faces for the first time, with their hoods off, so, yes, he must have understood. Maybe he was incredulous, for a moment he couldn't believe his Calvary would end like that, in a garage, in his pajamas, so anonymous, as though his killers were building attendants.

Maybe Aldo Moro sensed it from the very beginning, maybe he knew he had no options, no way out, that he was a pawn in a game he had once been master of, a man who knew power inside out, who knew how to use people, how to move them here and there.

Same day, May 9, 1978, near the Cinisi train station, Sicily. Dawn. Giuseppe Impastato[7]

They stuffed him with TNT and blew him up on the tracks near the station. Peppino Impastato watched them surround him, their faces exposed. He knew each one of them, all Mafia hands, the same men he'd been denouncing day after day from the microphone of his radio station.

He has no time to react, they're all over him, they insult him, beat him bloody.

Kicks bites fists boot heels rain down on him and there's more violence than necessary in the blows because these guys need to revenge themselves on him, on the one who dared to speak out, who had the courage to denounce them, and this is something they cannot tolerate. In their eyes, he now must become a thing, a thing to be squashed, to cancel out, a sack of fear to stuff with TNT the way you'd fill a sack of straw.

Now Peppino Impastato has passed out.

Yes, I want to believe that, that he passed out, that he couldn't feel his body dragged along those tracks behind the station close by his sleeping town, like through the stations of the cross.

Via Montalcini, in the garage

The terrorists are now face to face with Aldo Moro. Did they look each other in the eyes?

Did the first one to fire squeeze hard on the trigger?

Could he have stopped himself in that moment, not gone through with it?

Or not, or is it always the same, that by that point in the game the hands move on their own, like machines? But they tremble, they tremble! So you have to make them stronger, harder, you have to steel yourself, until you see before you not a man but a mere figure, a function of something, a thing. As though an order of destiny had to be followed, so the victim has to be just like that, defenseless, in his undershirt, maybe with a glimmer of trust in his eyes.

They fire. The burst feels like a liberation. They fire more than necessary, like in olden days when a sacrificial knife would go in and out, in and out of the victim. They fire. Aldo Moro is thrown backward from the violence of the blasts, so close. He raises his hands to his chest out of instinct, to protect himself. He falls, crumples.

On the ground, the body is already becoming a burden, a thing.

Now the terrorists conclude their sacrificial act, they dress him as though carrying out a hurried funeral rite because now time has started running again and everything is happening at once.

They dump him into the trunk of a car, a red Renault, then cover him with a blanket, but not entirely, the face is sticking out, disheveled, as if sleeping, like those people overwhelmed by infinite tiredness who collapse into sleep on the train home.

Cinisi, on the tracks

They drag him, push him, insult him, laugh like they were masters of the universe, like they held the destiny of man in their hands. They laugh.

No second thoughts on these sun-darkened faces. They're just carrying out a sentence someone else commanded, but they've got to take pleasure in doing it, they have to take their revenge against this intellectual, the cuckold, the communist, who blathered on the radio about Mafia and bribes.

An explosion will serve to make it clear who's in charge, the air has to resound, the earth vibrate. That way no one will hear that voice of his that talks, speaks out, denounces.

They leave him there on the tracks.

Peppino Impastato explodes with a boom, a cloud dismembers his body; now he can never be put back together again, he'll vanish, dematerialize, like he never existed.

Twenty-five years have passed since that May 9, 1978.

We all have fixed in our memory that image of Aldo Moro's supine body seen through the hatch door of that car, a red Renault.

No image has remained in our memory of Peppino Impastato, someone of my own generation, a comrade, someone who went to fight his battle in Sicily, among his own people, against the Mafia, and was murdered the same day as Aldo Moro. After twenty years, thanks to the confession of a penitent mafioso, we've finally found out that what we'd imagined was true, that Peppino Impastato was killed by the Badalamenti clan, the same one that Impastato denounced day after day from the microphones of his Radio Aut, in his daily campaign against disinformation.

In twenty years of efforts to hide their tracks, first they tried to pass him off as a suicide, then as a terrorist who was planting TNT, along the Cinisi line no less, a very busy route!

It took twenty years to get close to the truth.

What, on the other hand, do we know of Aldo Moro? Where, how, when, and who killed him, who kept him prisoner: it all seems so clear. But at the same time we feel and know that not everything has been said, that the truth is still far off, and that what is hidden is more troubling than what is visible. But over the years everyone's talked and written about the thick mud that covers those days, the unspoken truths, the unsolved mysteries, the blackmail. I'd like to tell a different story.

Because the fifty-five days of Moro's imprisonment were a watershed for a whole generation, my generation.

It was as though in those days there came to maturity a deep laceration that may have already existed, but only fully manifested itself, became visible, in that moment.

That's what I want to tell about, about what happened not only in the outside world, but inside me.

On March 16, 1978, I was twenty-eight, I'd been a father for a year and I'd been doing theater for four.

Via Fani

On March 16, 1978, when the radio started broadcasting about the attack in Via Fani and the kidnapping of Aldo Moro, I was getting out of my van to go grocery shopping in the open market in the Testaccio neighborhood in Rome. And I stopped there with the door open.

Right away, in those first moments, I was seized by excitement, a kind of euphoria.

I know, I could tell you something completely different, it wouldn't take much, with the wisdom of hindsight I could tell you I got angry when I heard the announcement on the radio, that I immediately condemned the action of the Red Brigades. No, that's not true, it didn't go like that.

I felt a sensation of exhilaration.

How was that possible? I'd always been far from the methods of struggle of the Red Brigades, I was never very convinced that the revolutionary struggle and the armed struggle necessarily had to coincide, and certainly not in that form, no. Despite all the changes in me in those years, how was it possible that, when I heard that radio announcement of the kidnapping, I felt that euphoric sense of belonging?

They'd kidnapped Moro! The president of the Christian Democrats. A symbol of power, of the *Palazzo* [Palace]![8] They'd struck a blow at the heart of the State, they'd really succeeded, it wasn't just a bunch of slogans.[9] How had they pulled it off? The undertaking was so impressive. "With geometric potency." The papers would write that: "with geometric potency."

And I wasn't the only one to be seized with that sense of excitement.

There were spontaneous assemblies in many universities, improvised marches where people yelled slogans that were then carved into city walls.

There were even social settings in which people toasted to what had happened.

But there were also demonstrations of just the opposite. Spontaneous strikes, others called by the unions, people who went into the streets to cry out against such provocations, in defense of democratic institutions.

The van's radio went on broadcasting the first reactions of the politicians, the comments from the halls of Parliament. The fascist, Almirante, and the Republican, La Malfa, were already demanding capital punishment, there was talk of war, some said it was a blow to the heart of the State.[10]

Walking with my grocery bags among the market stalls, people were reacting in all different ways.

One guy was saying, "It's a provocation! You'll see, now they'll fill the streets with tanks, you watch, now the army's gonna take over."

Another one was yelling, "But why'd they grab Moro? They should have gotten Andreotti, or Cossiga!"[11]

But there was a woman at a fruit stand saying over and over, "But those five poor boys, they shouldn't have killed them like that."

Right, those five. In the first moment, that word, "kidnapping," the image of someone like Moro kidnapped, was stronger than anything else for me. It took me a while to assimilate the part about Moro's five bodyguards killed there in Via Fani.

By evening, anyway, my euphoria had already passed. What I'd heard in the market kept running through my head. Why Moro, of all people? Cossiga was the one whose name we wrote with a capital K and the Nazi double SS on the banners we carried in our marches.

In the general view, Moro was less a symbol of the *Palazzo* than a symbol of that Christian Democrat way of operating, with his sentences that went on forever and twisted back on themselves with unending qualifications. Moro was the one who always inaugurated the Levant Trade Fair.[12] Sure, he was also one of those who'd been part of almost every government coalition in those years, the one who in 1975, in the center-left coalition, had passed the Reale Law, a law that authorized police and *carabinieri* to shoot during roadblocks. But just the same, it didn't add up. Wasn't Moro the one who'd always been most open to the Left, most open to dialogue? Wasn't he the very one who was bringing the Communist

Party into the government? That very day, in fact, the new majority coalition was supposed to be launched. And they kidnapped him that same morning?

The next day, the two dailies most read by comrades in the Movement, *Il Manifesto* and *Lotta Continua*, took very clear positions harshly attacking the terrorists.[13]

Lotta Continua printed a headline: "The Moro Kidnapping: The Worst and Dirtiest Ploy On the Heads of Italian Proletariats."

And *Il Manifesto* went even further, saying, "The bloody kidnapping of Aldo Moro is the last act of a decade of massacres concealed by the State," as though to say that the Red Brigades had been manipulated by infiltrators.

Two days later, *L'Unità* came out with the headline: "Scorch the Earth Around the Terrorists." What did that mean? What was to be burned, the whole extra-parliamentary movement of those years?[14]

Sometimes I think this story could be told in a completely different way, as a conflict between fathers and sons. If you read carefully the biographies of the terrorists, you find that at the beginning of the armed struggle, most of them came from the communist movement in the factories, the traditional party sections, from anti-fascist families who had fought in the resistance. Or they came from the extremist Catholics, the militant Christian movement.

They came from two great churches. After all, don't you need a great faith to get to where you'll kill a man in the name of a higher ideal of justice?

Perhaps our youth, in those years, was too full of God, that's right, too much faith, and the fathers became afraid of it, they closed the door on dialogue, on confrontation, maybe because our attitudes reminded them of how they'd been twenty years earlier. It was one wall against another. So to make themselves heard, the children began yelling louder and louder, until it led to a scream fired from a gun. I don't know, that might be another way to tell the same story. A way of understanding my reaction, for example, the reaction of someone who by then had quit direct political action, but kept on with it through theater, working in the outer neighborhoods, with children at risk, in the prisons, doing militant theater with deep commitment, a commitment I still believe in today, maybe that's how it was possible that at the first radio announcement, just in that initial moment, I was seized by a sensation of revolutionary excitement. Is that a contradiction? Yes, and that's exactly what I want to tell about.

Roadblock

A few days after the attack on Via Fani, must have been March 21, me, my companion Maria, and our son were driving along Via Gregorio Settimo in our beat-up yellow Fiat 500. One of its doors was white, replaced at a junkyard after an accident, you had to hold it with one hand while you were driving or else it would fly open.

At the bridge over the Tiber there's a roadblock; by this time there's hundreds of them around the city. The *carabinieri* are holding machine guns, they make us get out, they push us around while pointing the guns at us, they yank us, they frisk Maria to see whether maybe she's hiding a weapon instead of holding a baby.[15]

My son Mirto, barely a year old, immediately starts crying.

They open the hood, throw open the doors, fold down the seats, dump Maria's purse out on the ground; a baby bottle filled with milk rolls on the sidewalk, I start to bend over to pick it up but I can't, my legs go stiff from fear.

I look at the *carabinieri*, they're all younger than I am. I see how easy it would be for one of those guns to go off, the way they fling them around like that. Just like that, they could shoot and we'd be dead on the pavement, and the law would be on their side. That's the Reale Law, now I see it in front of me, concrete, tangible.

Luckily they shove us back into the car, angry they can't find anything.

Mirto is still crying and after a little while I notice that I'm driving with my hands clamped on the steering wheel with my back arched in the seat.

"Being hated makes you hate," said Pasolini. Yes, that's true, there was hate in their eyes, but there was also something else, a kind of impotence, a barely contained rage, not only because of the attack against the state, but because five of their comrades had been massacred. It was their sense of belonging to a corps, the corps of *carabinieri*, that was what had been violated and now they wanted revenge, quickly, right now, except they didn't know what to do, how to behave, they were bewildered, and so they acted out, dumping their anger on people like us.

Weapons

During those days, every time I went into a café or got on a bus, seeing all those jeeps going back and forth, whole neighborhoods searched, helicopters forever whirling over our heads, something rose in me. . . . I don't know if fear is the right word for it, a sense of uneasiness, uncertainty, a sensation that stuck to me like a second suit of clothes, another skin wrapping me, impalpable, thin, quotidian.

On March 25 the second Red Brigades communiqué had come out. They said they were interrogating Aldo Moro and would soon announce to the world the whole truth about those thirty years of Christian Democrat rule.

One of those nights I was alone at home with my son sleeping in the other room. Maria wasn't there, she'd gone to Florence with the other women in the theater group to perform at a demonstration in favor of abortion rights.

I couldn't sleep. The last news report of the night had shown again that same photo of Moro taken by the Red Brigades in his cell.

I couldn't imagine someone like Moro imprisoned. What was he thinking about just then?

It was also strange that I was having such thoughts. When Judge Sossi had been kidnapped in '74, nothing about him touched me.[16] This time, instead, seeing that photograph, the face of Aldo Moro in front of the symbol of the Red Brigades, with that white cowlick in his hair, that face I'd been indifferent to, or, rather adversarial toward, the face of a priest, now, to see him like that, imprisoned, now that face looked me over as though I were responsible for his confinement.

A few days earlier they'd held the funerals for Moro's five bodyguards massacred in Via Fani, and every so often the television would repeat the images of their bullet-riddled bodies lying among the cars.

I was especially struck by the one on the ground with his arms wide open, in a cross shape. He looked like a kid. And there was that other one who had thrown his body forward to protect Moro.

I'd seen a lot of pictures of murdered bodies in those years. Lots. But this time was different, I don't know why. It was as if all the others that I had tried to cancel from my memory had now come back all together, all of them, all those murdered in cold blood as they left their homes or walked down the steps at the university, all the victims with no way out, without a chance for a fair fight, all those killings I could never find a good reason for.

How had we come to this? How'd it happen that friends, comrades from my political group, from the marches, had suddenly started talking about weapons? From one day to the next they started using technical terms from specialized magazines, as though they were infatuated with weapons. But wasn't it always the fascists who loved guns?

But now, instead, I was looking at that photograph of that young man in Milan wearing that balaclava, holding that pistol with his arms forward like some secret agent in an American film . . . weapons.[17]

Weapons.

Maybe when the state had decreed that tire irons and wrenches were to be considered weapons, maybe some comrade in the Movement thought, "If they're all weapons, then I'm better off with a gun." If you really thought about it, the signs had been there some time too.

All you had to do was be in a political group as it prepared for a demonstration and you noticed that by now the most important part was all about the *servizio d'ordine*, how to organize ourselves, how to defend ourselves, what weapons to bring.

But what could you do, if the police went around dressed as students during the protests, holding pistols in their hands to provoke the crowds? What could you do if they shot tear gas canisters at your head during marches? Isn't that how they killed Francesco Lorusso in Bologna? And Giorgiana Masi in Rome, on the Garibaldi Bridge?[18]

What were we supposed to do, with fascists blowing up innocent people with bombs, maybe assisted by the secret police, like in the massacre in Piazza Fontana in Milan or in Piazza della Loggia in Brescia?[19] What were we supposed to do? When did the clash turn so harsh, when did it get out of control, when? When did people start talking about open warfare?

Demonstration

I remember a demonstration in Rome at the beginning of '71, it was cold, must have been the end of January or beginning of February, a huge march that went down Via Nazionale from Piazza Esedra, comrades everywhere, many walking behind banners representing political groups but lots also just there on their own, loose. The march worked its way along slowly, powerful, festive. Yeah, there was still that '68 feeling, as we walked people competed to come up with the most original chants. Halfway along I was already hoarse from yelling. Passing under the windows of the bourgeoisie, it made you feel so great to scream up at them.

Also, I was walking along holding Carla's hand, and after the demonstration I was hoping to go back to her place and hold all of her.

When we got to Largo Chigi, the police were already deployed as we'd expected.

We start chanting the usual slogans with our fists raised: "Killer Cops! Killer Cops!"

All of a sudden from behind the march, someone throws a Molotov cocktail that shatters in front of the police line, the fire flares up fast, the police charge. There's a scream in the crowd, Carla is thrown to the ground by the shoving mass fleeing every which way. I help her get up, we plug our mouths with handkerchiefs, our eyes tearing from the gas that's hit the ground right next to us, the gas is poisoning us and we start running through a little street toward the Pantheon. After a moment I notice that Carla's not at my side anymore, I turn to look for her and see a whole bunch of comrades are following me! Like I knew where I was going! My friend Fabio comes up, he's a committed pacifist and he yells, "Did you see those assholes with the Molotovs, now look what they've got us into!" But I can't answer because I see that down on the other side, at the end of the street, there's a squad of riot cops advancing against us with their shields up, so I turn and gesture to the others to change direction, like that, just by intuition. Now Fabio is just ahead of me, we're running like mad with our eyes burning, I can hear the teargas canisters whistling past but I don't turn back anymore, I run, nothing but run, hurdling the parked cars, scrambling over them. Fabio has already turned the corner, but as soon as I get there I stop in my tracks, there's a riot going on in front of me, the cops have surrounded a bunch of comrades, it's hand-to-hand combat, I dive for cover behind a Volkswagen, and through the teargas fumes I can see the clubs of the cops raising up and raining down on the people on the ground five, six, seven times. Fuck, that's Fabio on the ground! I recognize his t-shirt!

I see a cop spin and kick Fabio hard in the kidneys, now I jump out into the open, I'm seized with blind rage, I'm about to throw myself into the rumble when I see our *servizio d'ordine* arrive wearing helmets and carrying Molotovs, they're about to launch them, and I, I too scream with the others, and I grab a Molotov on the fly, and throw it, my Molotov, it smashes on a bench near the jeep. The cops beat a retreat, we help the injured get up off the ground, Fabio is holding his side, he stumbles, vomits, but manages to stay on his feet. The confusion is incredible, there's smoke everywhere, a paving stone thrown by some asshole gets me in the ankle, I scream with pain. Now it's Fabio who's holding me and dragging me away; my ankle is bleeding, I limp. Fabio takes me into a church, we go to the holy water stoup, he makes the sign of the cross and then pushes me into the aisle on the left, the darkest spot. The sounds outside are muffled in here, they sound far off, we kneel at a pew so we don't stand out, Fabio hides his long hair inside the collar of his shirt, I can't follow what's happening anymore, there's the smell of incense, I'm kneeling there with my ankle pounding with pain, my hand still feels the weight of the Molotov I just threw. I'm just sorry I didn't hit the jeep. I should have hit the jeep, a few more meters and I would have . . . but at the same time this anger rises up in me, anger against those with the Molotovs who threw us into the middle of it and left us there like this. Fuck them and what they call their "leap forward in the quality of the struggle."

Eh, but the next time they wouldn't screw me, the next time I wouldn't show up unprepared at a demonstration, the next time . . .

What was I thinking? Now I had to get a gun too?

Giorgio

After the first communiqués from the Red Brigades were found in Rome, any time you rushed out of a phone booth or dropped some papers into a public trash bin, everyone would suddenly stare at you like they thought you might be a terrorist. It was as though an invisible city had been laid over the visible one of our daily lives, an invisible spiderweb made up of crisscrossing threads, ambush points, new encounters with death. And for the members of the Red Brigades, this invisible network was absolutely visible. They knew how to move around in it, where to go, they lived inside a magic net made of numbers, streets, telephones, meeting times and places. It was the world around the net that became uncertain, unstable.

Especially for people like me. Yes, for me more than others, because I could almost picture their meetings, I could almost intuit the thought growing in their minds. After all, how many similar meetings had we held in the early '70s, where we used the same words, the same arguments, that revolutionary lexicon, yeah, I could almost see them shut up in their clandestine rooms, cut off from real contact with the world, where after talking and talking and talking among themselves for days and days, you actually come to believe that you're the avant-garde of the world of the future.

Then you go out and shoot.

On April 3 there'd been a giant police round-up, lots of comrades had been jailed.

That same night, Luisa phoned to remind me that the next day was the anniversary of the death of Giorgio, and that his mother wanted everyone over to her house, all Giorgio's old friends and comrades, for a big dinner. Luisa warned me that some friends wouldn't be there because of the round-up, but the dinner was going to happen no matter what.

Giorgio. The year before, at the beginning of April '77, I'd opened the newspaper and saw Giorgio's photo on page one, I'd stopped there stock still at the bar of the café by my house, unable to utter a sound.

We'd been militants together in the same political group in the early '70s, Giorgio was much younger than me, he was still in high school, but we'd become great friends anyway. I liked his way of doing things, that contagious willingness to take on anything. Giorgio was one of those people whose eyes sparkle when they talk, always full of enthusiasm, always ready to give his all for others. But now there he was in the paper, in a photograph like a mug shot.

The *carabinieri* had killed him right after a robbery.

The robbery was totally improvised. Yes, often in those years, it happened that the youngest ones, Giorgio must have been twenty by then, felt driven to demonstrate to the senior terrorists, the chiefs, just how totally committed they were, by springing a bank robbery maybe, to provide money for the struggle.

It was like an entrance exam.

The *carabinieri* had stopped them right after the robbery. They'd gotten out of their car with their arms raised, having left their weapons in the trunk.

But when Giorgio had reached his hand into his jacket for his ID card, the *carabinieri*, just as young as Giorgio, reacted with fear and started shooting wildly; Giorgio took a direct hit at the first blast and died just like that.

When I arrive at his mother's house the night of the anniversary, I see Luisa's already there. She leads me into another room to show me an album she's put together of photos of Giorgio. She wants me to see them.

With effort, I say okay. I start turning the pages of the album.

The first photo shows Giorgio and Luisa in each other's arms, at the beach at Ostia.

In another photo, Giorgio has just finished painting a banner for a demonstration. He's standing there all proud in his parka, brush in hand. Behind him the banner reads, "THE BOURGEOIS STATE WON'T CHANGE, BRING IT DOWN."

The last photo shows Giorgio in the middle of a group of friends standing outside the neighborhood movie house. Someone's reaching up two fingers behind his head to make it look like he has horns.

A few steps from that movie house was the headquarters where all the local political groups would meet. I remember an assembly there toward the end of '72, a meeting like many others held in those months, in those years, every one crucial, every one decisive, bad news not to be there. The day's agenda was about occupying abandoned buildings or fighting evictions, I forget which.

I wanted to go mainly to see comrades I hadn't seen for a while, people like Giorgio, but especially Sara. Gorgeous Sara. Everyone was after her, and me too, though I had little hope, she seemed unreachable. But I thought I'd give it a try anyway, I'd go to the assembly meeting and if I saw her there, I'd invite her to the movies. "Make it or break it," I told myself.

When I enter the big room, it's already filled with comrades, we all greet one another, hugs and kisses, and there's Giorgio; he pulls me into a crushing embrace, and in the back I see Sara's there too.

I liked the big assemblies most of all.

You could feel this vital energy going off in all different directions, there wasn't that sense of maintaining homogeneity at all costs, even though everyone there believed more or less the same thing, that the revolution was nigh and the world was about to change totally, from one day to the next.

When I took part in the smaller meetings, on the other hand, where you worked out a specific course of action, I always felt sort of out of place. To be part of the group, you had to read certain books and not read others, you had to memorize certain Maoist-Leninist quotations —it was a little hard to take. Because of this the others didn't count on me too much. When it came down to it, to them I was just a stray dog. That was the term, those who weren't within a specific group were "stray dogs." They only looked for me when they needed someone to light up the crowd, because I could speak well, otherwise they never called me.

As soon as the meeting begins, you can tell from the first comments that the printed agenda isn't going to be followed and there's some other plan at work.

The leaders of all the different groups take turns speaking, but they're all using a particular language and tone of voice more appropriate for a rally than a planning meeting.

I remember looking over toward my friend Paolo, seated at some distance, and he looked back at me with the same expression, disbelieving and a little lost. The voices of the speakers were getting still louder and more shrill, they were saying a decisive phase had arrived, simple activism wasn't enough anymore, the kinds of phrases often used to warm people up for a demonstration. But it was different this time, as though a hidden thread connected all the various statements, there was an urgency, some decision had to be made right now, but it wasn't going to be about occupying a building, there was something else in the air that raised the tension in the room and riled the crowd.

At a certain point Riccardo P. gets up to speak, one of the rising leaders, a spellbinding orator I knew well because he came from the same political group Giorgio and I were in years before. With an inspired voice he starts saying we've come to a decisive moment, we have to make a leap forward in the quality of the political-revolutionary struggle, that now's the time, comrades, to create a new form of political-military structure. Then, raising his voice to the limit, "Comrades, the moment has come for all of us to go underground, here and now, comrades, so if you're willing to go underground, raise your hand!"

Underground?

That word meant changing my life from one day to the next, vanishing from sight, moving around Rome carrying guns, ready to shoot and kill. Underground meant living inside iron rules, rigid and military.

Raise my hand?

There was general euphoria in the room, I saw almost everyone stand up with their hands in the air, the youngest made the P38 gesture with their hands, there was Giorgio too, with the whole group of high school students.[20] I didn't raise my hand, but it was more because I was stunned than because I understood what was going on. I turned toward Paolo and saw that he too was still seated, along with a few others scattered here and there.

Sara, no, she was standing there, her face glowing, with her hand up in the P38 gesture, and when she turned to look at me and saw I was still seated, her expression clouded over with scorn. The meeting ended almost immediately. The chiefs were taking names of volunteers, setting up secret meetings for the coming days, talking together in low voices. I suddenly felt left out, I got up feeling ashamed and Paolo, me, and the others walked out into the Roman night shocked and confused, not speaking.

Riccardo

A strange encounter I'd had in the summer of '72 came to mind, and only now did I realize its meaning.

I used to go to the beach whenever I could at Torvaianica, just beyond Ostia. I remember that people had built unauthorized shacks there, at first to sell snacks, and they'd slowly grown into restaurants or beach-umbrella renters: it was a free beach, never crowded.

There was a place called "GUERRINO ER MARINARO" where you could eat well for cheap, the specialty was spaghetti with clams that fat old Guerrino himself, who maybe had really been a sailor way back in the past, raked out of the sand every day at dawn, standing there in the surf up to his belt.

I was stretched out on the beach reading when I see Riccardo P. coming up to me along the strand.

He was in a swimsuit, tall, bigger than me, a charismatic type much adored by flocks of women militants.

Our extra-parliamentary political groups had fused some months before, after an infinite series of meetings and documents announcing our goals.

Riccardo was always in the front row, generous to the point of self-sacrifice, willing to take on any problem, to be everywhere at once, a real political Stakhanovite, he had this way of orating at meetings that was almost a caricature, like a revolutionary from the 1800s, a take-off on Santorre di Santarosa.[21]

What struck me about him was the utter faith with which he proclaimed the rightness of his political line, which had to be followed blindly; he was able to sweep people along behind him, the youngest ones especially were entranced by his style.

As for me, he tried my patience a little. He was too baroque, too bombastic, he never got to the point but would leap instead onto slogans and proclamations, deeply felt and sincere no doubt, but hurled suddenly like lightning bolts from the blue after a long speech that just twisted around itself with neither head nor tail.

Or maybe I distrusted him because he came from a rich background, scion of a wealthy family.

Since I'd always lived in scrubby working-class neighborhoods like Acilia, on the far outskirts of Rome, closer to lumpenproletariat sentiments of hostility and anarchism, I instinctively distrusted those well-bred types, they didn't convince me.

Maybe I secretly envied their status, that way they could pull off going around without a penny in their pocket and get other people to cover their part of the bill after meals, with this attitude as though they were above vile money. Riccardo told me he'd called my house and they told him I was here at the beach so he'd decided to come find me.

Without giving me time to answer he launched off on one of his sermons, a veiled critique of my conduct, like he was my big brother or something, telling me how I'd been letting down the cause recently.

He asked me where I'd been, how the campaign was going in the occupied houses, he said he thought the way I operated followed political fashion too much. He went on like that, from topic to topic, as if we were in a private meeting in our group office instead of taking the sun at the beach.

I still hadn't recovered from my surprise at finding him there, the two of us together who'd shared at most a couple of dinners after meetings, a car trip or two to Milan for a demonstration, nothing more than that, since we were separated both by age and upbringing.

I was uncomfortable, and he must have noticed it because he switched to making jokes about the bodies of the girls parading by, but it was forced, as though he wanted to show off what a regular, funny guy he was. Then he suggested we take a dip. I didn't want to so he went in by himself, with that impeccable Tarzan style of his, he comes back dripping and without toweling off he stretches out next to me and starts over again about politics and programs, asking my thoughts once in a while about this or that matter, staring at me intently as though he really wanted to find out what I was thinking.

I was confused, the situation was so strange, my only reaction was a pervasive sense of guilt for my inadequate answers.

I could tell, though, that he was truly curious about me, I could feel that in his own way he admired my abilities, the charisma I exercised over the comrades. Smiling, he called them "the confused ones," the ones who can't stand organized meetings, so he starts praising me for the work I'd done the year before during the occupation of the university building, for the contacts I'd established with political committees in the outer neighborhoods, in Ostia and Casal Palocco. Then he stopped to take a breath, as though coming to the end of a long preamble leading to the real subject.

He began in an impassioned voice to say that he now felt a decisive turning point was coming up, that the system's repression was growing day by day, that it was no longer tolerable to live this way, one day at a time. I agreed, didn't I?

It wasn't enough anymore just to announce a plan or a political line, it was time to accelerate, something more was needed, couldn't I feel it in the air?

As he said it, his eyes swept over the horizon, his expression said he could really smell something in the air that I still couldn't, however hard I tried. Suddenly, he gathered up a fistful of sand and let it run out through his fingers like an hourglass, staring at it, hypnotized.

"You know, my son has started calling me papà?"

This threw me, what was going on? There was something in that sudden change that troubled me, made me nervous. I didn't say anything for a while, surely for too long. I didn't know what to say, then I mumbled something about how I promised to come to the next round of meetings, but it was obvious I didn't mean it.

As though he realized he'd exposed too much of himself, as though he'd given in somehow by revealing a personal side of himself, he picked up the book I was reading. It was *Moby Dick* in Pavese's translation.[22] A sort of sacred book for me, a Bible I was rereading that summer for maybe the third time. "So you think you're going to make a revolution with this?" he remarked with a bitter smile. "What the fuck are you doing here sunbathing when there are comrades busting their asses in the factories, getting cut to pieces every day, don't you see what's going on around you, these people, this . . ."

He made a gesture that included the whole horizon in his disgust, everything, from the sea to the sand, as though the whole day had suddenly become useless and senseless.

He was done now, he looked around as though gasping for air, his arms wide in the air tracing arcs as though he wanted to cancel out everything he could see, he turned to me, face to face.

"Come on, Marco! Come on! The time is now! Don't let yourself go!"

He realized he'd spoken too loudly and people were looking at him, so he added in a conspiratorial tone, "You don't want to give up now," he said, clutching my shoulder. "We're waiting for you, we need comrades like you!"

He got dressed quickly, finding a phony, playful tone, then waved and headed back to the parking lot and his motorcycle.

I was stunned. I picked up the book he'd tossed aside. Of everything he'd said what hurt me most was that *Moby Dick* was useless.

Several seconds earlier, for a moment, I'd felt a destructive, nihilistic rage pouring out of him.

I watched him walk away, he didn't limp like Ahab with his whalebone peg leg but you could still see a kind of battle fatigue setting in.

When he'd talked to me about his son his voice had changed, it became softer, so different from his harsh scorn. Yes, with such destructive energy he would have dragged anyone down a black hole, but I'd never seen a will so steely and at the same time so weak. The day was over. I got dressed very slowly. A few kids had made a sand castle and were shrieking, happy and frightened of the approaching waves.

I learned only later, a long time later, that it was during those days that Riccardo was trying to decide whether or not to join the *lotta armata*, the armed struggle.

When he came looking for me at the beach I don't know how far he was in making that decision. Maybe he was already well on his way and his questions had been more about me than him, a sort of test to see if I could make the same choice he was making. It had partly been like that. He'd come to test me and he must have been bitterly disappointed and probably thought I was lost to the cause. Since I was completely unaware of what he was really asking me, my answers must have been frustrating and irritating.

And still there had been moments when his gaze betrayed a nostalgic feeling of belonging, to that beach and to any other day like the one we were living, a feeling of someone stuck on loving the very things he knew he was about to lose.

Riccardo was arrested a few years later, after becoming a wanted criminal for a while. He'd been wounded in a shootout.

He ended up in prison, attempted escape, participated in a few riots inside.

I'm sure that he found an attentive audience on the inside who nurtured his constant state of rebellion.

Armando

April 15: the sixth communiqué from the Red Brigades is issued. Aldo Moro is sentenced to death.

The Movement is now split into three factions. There are those who still defend or in some way justify the Red Brigades, calling them *compagni che sbagliano*, "comrades in error." Then there are those who believe that the secret services have infiltrated the Brigades and are maneuvering them.

But there's another part of the Movement that has started to think that the real issue now is different, it is finding any means possible to negotiate Moro's freedom.[23]

And I agree with them.

What was I thinking?

It was as if, with each day that passed, there was no Christian Democrat dignitary in that people's prison anymore. The more communiqués, the more ultimatums, the more everything seemed to seize up, the more it seemed like we were acting out a script that had already been written, in which the victim had never had any hope for escape.

The more these sorts of thoughts came to me and the more political actions that took place, the more it seemed to me that Aldo Moro was a man just like any other, a man like me, one you couldn't let just croak like that, he was a man to save, to save, that's all.

One day in late April I went to see Armando in jail.

It was my turn in the rotation his friends had organized and I hadn't seen him in more than two months.

I make it through the usual security checkpoints, one gate after another that the guards let crash behind you so that you can feel how pissed off they are, too, to be shut up in here. I reach the visitors' room, filthy as usual.

Armando's already there, waiting for me. He looks pale and worn out to me but I don't say anything, we exchange the usual words and greetings and he asks me right away about Lucia, his wife, and his daughter Alice. I tell him what I've heard, that they're fine.

And just to start a conversation I ask if he's been reading the papers about the Moro Affair and what he thinks about it, but he lifts his hand as if to say he could care less and abruptly, changing tone, starts talking enthusiastically about the land he's got in Umbria, about the farmhouse and that he's decided to rehab everything as soon as he leaves here, in fourteen months. That's what he says, he doesn't say a year and two months, he says fourteen months.

Armando is serving three years on a bum rap?

One night the doorbell rings and when he opens the door he finds an old friend, a guy he hasn't seen in a long time, someone who had sort of taken himself out of circulation. By that time Armando was spending all his time working in the hospital.

The guy asks if Armando will keep a package for him overnight, something wrapped up in newspaper inside a plastic bag, just for the night, maybe in his basement. Armando doesn't know what to do, Lucia's out, the comrade is insisting, saying he can't wander around Rome with the thing on him, tries to hint at what it might be but Armando doesn't want to know any more details.

"C'mon, why do you even care, it's only for a night, worse comes to worst I'll be back for it tomorrow, I swear."

Armando goes down to the basement. It doesn't take a genius to figure out what he has in his hands: through the paper and plastic he can feel the contours and weight of what he's taking down there.

Two days go by and nobody comes to the house. Armando didn't say anything to Lucia, and every once in a while he goes down in the basement, like he wants to hide the plastic bag just a little better.

At dawn on the third day Armando's house is surrounded by the *carabinieri*.

They yank them out of bed, search the place and know immediately where to look: in the basement they find the weapon and Armando is screwed.

He'll never know for sure exactly what happened. There's some story of a robbery done by some inexperienced comrades, a caper by a gang of desperadoes from the neighborhood that didn't come off.

Right after they're arrested these guys start talking and maybe to cut a better deal they lay it on thicker and give up his name. Anyway, Armando is tried summarily and gets three years. And he should count himself lucky the gun was never fired. Now he just wants everyone to drop the subject.

Lucia has never forgiven him. She spent three months in jail herself trying to prove her innocence. And this is the thing that eats away at him in jail, the thing that he most obsesses about.

Finally the time for the visit ends. Yes, "finally" because when I get up to leave I almost feel a sense of relief. After the last gate shuts behind me I turn to wave to Armando. He's still standing there, but he doesn't wave back. And for a second I feel kind of guilty because I'm lucky enough not to be shut up in there.

When I get on the 44 bus I'm still a little stunned and as it lumbers up the Janiculum Hill I give a start all of a sudden because I thought I saw a comrade up by the bus driver. But I'm wrong. This is paranoia, because there's nobody I know anywhere near the driver.

But if there had been? What if I really had recognized an old comrade there on the bus, one of those who'd disappeared, someone on the lam, I do know some of them, don't I? Someone maybe with whom I'd picketed or, maybe even more, a real friend, what would I do? Would I wave?

And what if that same day near the stop where he gets off, close to Piazza Ottavilla, someone was murdered—it wouldn't take much to connect the dots—what would I do then?

Let's say that tonight something happens to me, tonight when I'm alone in the house, like Armando. Somebody rings the bell. I open the door and find Sara. Gorgeous Sara.

I imagine her even more beautiful now than before, certainly more womanly. She starts talking to me without revealing too much, she knows I already know everything about her anyway, and then all of a sudden she asks if she can stay the night. She asks me like it's a given, like something comrades do for each other. She asks me with that same scornful gaze from that time at the meeting.

Now, despite all the possibilities I could imagine, when I think of this scene I'm paralyzed. I don't know what to do. I stand there in the doorway. It would take only one step backward, as if to invite her in, and I'd be complicit, I don't even know in what. If instead I closed the door and they arrested her that same night, for the rest of my life I would feel responsible. So I just stand there, unable to choose, letting the time to decide lengthen infinitely. Neither here nor there.

"Neither with the Red Brigades nor with the State."

When this slogan had appeared in the headlines of *Lotta Continua* it seemed so perfectly coined, an ideal escape route, a way not to get screwed in that duel.[24] We weren't siding with the Red Brigades and their methods but we weren't siding with the State either, the State that continued bumping off students and workers in piazzas all over Italy. We weren't taking sides, it was simple, neither here nor there. Neither with the Red Brigades nor with the State.

It seemed like such a liberating option.

But now, more than thirty days after Moro's kidnapping, that sentence struck me as a sign of impotence.

There's a Truffaut film, *The Woman Next Door* [1981], with Gérard Depardieu and Fanny Ardant.

In the film he's a married man, settled, with a wife and kids.

One day he sees an old flame who has moved into the building and who's also married. They start to see each other again secretly, pretty soon they find out they still love each other, and they keep on seeing each other until they get found out. A scandal erupts. She's forced to move with her husband and their apartment stays vacant, and everything seems to revert to the way it was before.

But one night Depardieu can't fall asleep. He hears the door of the apartment next door open and shut, brushing against the doorframe. He gets out of bed and sees that the apartment's door is ajar and that she's waiting for him in an empty room. They embrace, roll around on the floor, they start making love and just as they start to come she takes a gun out of her purse and shoots first him and then herself.

In the next scene, as the funeral procession passes, you hear the voiceover. One of the friends they had in common says what could be written on their headstones: "Neither with you nor without you."

Today I ask myself whether the whole Movement in those days didn't commit suicide in the same way, all embracing the same beloved cause that had given it birth and raised it.

Newspapers

The eighth communiqué from the Brigades comes out April 24. It reads, "The price for Aldo Moro's destiny is the liberation of political prisoners."

The margins for negotiation are getting slimmer all the time.

In his letters from his prison, Moro sends out desperate appeals to the Christian Democrat officials, but no one budges.[25]

The non-negotiation front, contrary to any prior practice with terrorists, doesn't give in. Everything collapses.

Those days, whenever I went into the kitchen to open the fridge, I saw Aldo Moro's face looking out at me.

It had been Antonio, an Argentine who lived with us and worked in our theater group, who had taped the famous photo of Moro in the people's prison to the fridge door. With a marker he'd written, riffing Pirandello, "One, no one, one hundred thousand" and patiently, one after the other, he'd stuck a series he'd cut out of the papers of adjectives that journalists used trying to describe Moro's complex personality: Moro the melancholic, the mysterious, the meek Moro, clear, slow, tactful, a calm Moro, solitary, proud, optimistic, pessimistic, reticent, hieratic, patient.[26]

Beneath "patient," Antonio had drawn an arrow with a marker that pointed to a cartoon by Andrea Pazienza: it showed a police inspector throwing open the door of an apartment pointing a finger and inquiring "Aldo Moro?" The tenant stood there, frightened and with his arms raised, and answered, "No, [I'm] blond and short."[27]

Antonio thought that we ought to be able to laugh about this Moro Affair, otherwise we'd be crushed, that in Argentina he'd seen a lot of bad stuff, much worse than Moro. In his view you needed to grasp the grotesqueries of the situation. So he had papered the walls of the kitchen with cartoons and illustrations cut out of the papers. Near the dish drainer there was a drawing of a huge rooster crouched as though he were sitting on a nest made of the city's rooftops.[28]

In those days there was an obsession with nests or lairs, the police found them, the Brigades' hideouts, everywhere, one day they found them and the next they didn't, the hideouts were always there but the Brigades never were, except for the real hideouts, like the one in Via Gradoli, that never got searched nor unearthed even if they were brought to the attention of the authorities.[29]

In this drawing you saw this rooster sitting on a nest and he had this machine gun tucked under one arm and on his chest he wore the five-pointed star of the Brigades and the dialogue bubble coming out of his beak said, "Here I hatch, there I hatch, everywhere I hatch-hatch."

Maybe Antonio was right: grotesqueries happened every day. But maybe we needed a buffer zone to be able to identify them.

Just a few days before, just a little ways away, in Via di Villa Pamphili, the police had stopped a student on a scooter at a checkpoint.

After they checked his ID, the police gestured for him to raise the seat and open the tank so that they could check inside. The student raised the seat, opened the tank, looked around and said, "Come on out, Aldo, they got us!"

He was tried summarily and sentenced to six months in jail.

But the most absurd news item had appeared on the cover of a weekly magazine.

It had to do with the expert analysis of a noted psycho-graphologist. Basing his analysis on the Brigades' letters, this fellow had analyzed the way they wrote and his detailed reading led him to the following conclusion: that the Brigades were to be understood psychoanalytically as rooted exclusively in the oral phase.

Those in the Freudian oral phase have serious problems with their mothers in early childhood. It is for this reason that they constantly seek symbols that can act as substitutes for the lacking maternal figure. They therefore love water, the symbol of maternity par excellence, or better still the sea, the Great Mother.

Since they were in the oral phase, they were also in constant need of something to put in their mouths, to nibble on, cookies, sweets, soft drinks; in short they needed free access to cafés.

At this point it seemed like it would work if you analyzed the cash register receipts for the cafés on the Roman seaside and once you had discovered a café that had seen some increase in activity during Moro's sequester, the jig was up. Just a stone's throw away you would be sure to find Moro's prison, with Moro and his wardens inside.

And the great thing is that the agents of law and order had actually tried it.

If today you reread those articles by journalists, politicians, psychologists, the scenario is more than grotesque, it's sinister. They had staged Moro's funeral prior to his death. From the start of the arrival of those letters from the people's prison everyone rushed to prove that he couldn't have written them.

"The handwriting is rather ambiguous."

"Those aren't his words."

"The signature is his, but certainly not the content."

"The handwriting is his but the letter has no value, he's writing under the effect of hypnosis."

"The handwriting is child-like."

"An unrecognizable Moro."

"But is it the true Moro or another Moro?"

"We have never believed anything he wrote in his letters."

The more Moro tried to communicate, to make himself understood, to find some solution, the more all those around him rushed to discredit him, to pass him off as not of sound mind.

In this way, all those members of the non-negotiation front that refused to bargain had to play the game of not hearing Moro's voice in their heads; it didn't matter anyway, he wasn't the one writing the letters.

The most coherent of all of these was, from the start, Indro Montanelli.[30] Even from the very first letter sent to Zaccagnini, Moro was, in Montanelli's view, politically dead. In one of his last articles in the *Giornale* he had declared that "Aldo Moro, the president of the Christian Democrat Party, died the very second he was kidnapped.[31] He can be held responsible for nothing that he said or did afterward. The only respect that we can and should pay to him is to mark March 16 as the date of his disappearance. The rest should be left in silence."

Petrosinella

In the first days of May we have to go perform in an elementary school.

We're already there by 8:30 and we begin to unload the costume trunks and our instruments. Pietro is the school custodian.

After some brief conversation and not a second after learning we're comrades in the Movement, he runs to the principal's office and comes back with the front page of *L'Unità* to show us, with the article in hand, that the PCI is right to side with the non-negotiators and that it is clear that the Brigades are just provocateurs and that folks like us who want to negotiate are simply playing the Brigades' game. I can't take it anymore and I tell him that it's actually the PCI that fails to understand anything, that they have gotten caught up in this fable of non-negotiation, and don't they see that they're ending up supporting a government that's worse than the center-left one that came before it? But Pietro won't listen and keeps repeating this and that . . . I interrupt him, I really don't have the time to get into a conversation about this right now, the show is about to start, the children are all seated and Maria is giving me the go-ahead to go on stage.

Maria plays the part of Petrosinella in the story, which was actually our version of *Little Miss Parsley*.[32] In the story she is captured and held prisoner by three terrible witches. I am Memé, the witches' cousin. I have magical powers, too, but they are limited, and in the first scene I fall madly in love with Petrosinella and decide to betray my kin and help the maiden by giving her three magic objects, a broom, an ax, and a piece of bread, three very ordinary objects.

It's Petrosinella that will make them magical when she understands all by herself how to use them to succeed in the tests that are a part of all fairy tales.

I have just given Petrosinella a kiss and handed over the three objects and I exit for a costume change. In the wings is Pietro, who just won't back down. He says that the State can't allow itself to bargain with criminals and then I tell how false that is because in wartime bargains have always been struck with enemies so that prisoners can be freed. "War? What war?" he asks. There's no war going on, he was part of the Resistance and he knows war when he sees it, we don't know what we're talking about. Then I start to tell him . . . but why bother? Pietro is unshakeable, he's proud that all the constitutional parties, the DC included, have lined up behind the PCI on the non-negotiation front. The DC the party of non-negotiation? C'mon, if there is one party that has no hard line, it is the DC. The only non-negotiable thing the DC has is its stranglehold on power, and as to the rest, they have always blown with the prevailing wind. It was convenient for them not to negotiate this time and to let the Brigades bump off Moro, that's how it was.

Just then I hear Maria say my cue and out of instinct I just come out of the wings but I realize that with all this talking to Pietro I haven't changed costume. At this point in the story I should appear in a huge mask and play the role of the ogre who lurks behind Petrosinella. But I am still dressed as Memé. Now what can I do? I make a monstrous grimace but the children laugh because they recognize me.

Luckily Maria picks up the ball and says, "Memé, why are you making that terrible face? Does your stomach hurt?" And the kids laugh even harder.

So I follow her lead and we improvise something that completely cracks them up.

What a wonder the theater is: you just need to switch up on the script a bit to end up going in a completely different direction.

At the end the children are all on their feet happy and clapping and the show is over. Petrosinella has successfully freed herself from jail. Fables always end happily.

We start to strike the set so we can pack it up when we see Pietro come back, somewhat diminished and sad and he wants to say goodbye, like comrades. Going toward the door he takes my elbow and says, "Y'know what? We're all tangled up in this game."

And this time he's right. It's true, we've all been tangled up in this game and it's as though you're playing cards, one of those games when in the end you can only play with the cards you've got, laying down cards that have already all been determined.

Address Book

May 9, 1978. They open the trunk of a car.

Aldo Moro's body becomes visible. This will be the last public image, then the photographs will endure, and they'll keep on talking to us in memory, like all images.

I look at that car. A Renault 4, *the* car of the '70s, the car of the Movement since it was fuel efficient and didn't cost much. You could often find them used and they passed from one person to another, the car of the Left, with that gear-shift that made it look like you were driving a tram, that broke your arm, with the shocks that made you feel like you were in a boat with every curve you took. We'd gone on our first road trips in that car, smoked our first joints, listened to music, always too many of us crowded on the uncomfortable seats.

I look at it now, and I see that in some way they took this, too, away from us. That car is now a hearse, and it's not only Aldo Moro's funeral that we're celebrating.

A few months later I am alone in the house, it's very late, it's hot and the windows are open. I'm at my desk and in front of me is my address book, coming apart at the seams. It's jammed with addresses, street names, telephone numbers. I pick it up and start turning the pages. On the black cover is the year I bought it. 1970. Eight years have passed.

I start with the letter A. I turn the first page, then the second, then the third. I light a match, bring it close to the pages and let them burn. Then I do it with other pages, B, C, D and at the letter P there's Peppino Impastato and the address for Radio Aut.

Slowly, I let all the other pages burn.

I so wish that my actions that night had been out of human cowardice, yes, that I had been seized by fear over possible connections to people who had become dangerous. That had happened too during this time: how many comrades had ended up inside for an address in someone's book? What I wanted was for that gesture to be a surrender. No, it wasn't like that, I was burning something else and I absolutely knew what it was. For all those who did not take up arms— and we were the majority—that was the time when we were slowly silenced.

It was as if being against violence, against the State, against that worldview didn't have any greater chance with words than it had with arms.

And yet we'd all come out of the same 1968, we all came out of the same need for equality, for justice, we all came out of the same grand dream.

Notes

1. Since the early 1970s, each organized protest—sit-in, demonstration, strike, or occupation—had a *servizio d'ordine*. This was a military-like security service created within the Student Movement to block insiders' agitation and to ensure the safety of the protesters from external attacks. The *servizio d'ordine* would often have fights with right-wing extremists and the police. On some occasions, the *servizio* had sharp clashes with left-wing extremist groups as well.

2. *Barone* has here been translated as "fat cat." As we note also in the appendix, relative to Franco Nasi's essay, both *barone* and "fat cat" are pejorative terms used to describe individuals operating within a system in which they feed parasitically off the work of others.

3. Avanguardia Operaia [Workers' Vanguard], Manifesto, Lotta Continua [Ongoing Struggle], and Potere Operaio [Labor Power] were extra-parliamentary groups of

the so-called Nuova Sinistra [New Left]. Often critical toward the Student Movement, these groups were all active in the late 1960s and early 1970s. Avanguardia Operaia had strong connections with factory workers and trade unions. Manifesto was founded by a group of intellectuals banned from the Communist Party for their opposition to the Soviet Union's politics of aggression in Eastern Europe. Lotta Continua was a communist revolutionary organization generated from a schism within the Student Movement that took place in Turin in 1969. Both Lotta Continua and Manifesto published their own official newspapers. Potere Operaio was the second organization that sprung from the 1969 Turin schism. A Leninist group connected with factory workers, it advocated mass revolution. In the second half of the 1970s, most of these groups converged under the umbrella of radical parliamentary parties such as the newly born Democrazia Proletaria [Proletarian Democracy] and Partito di Unità Proletaria [Party of Proletarian Unity], which earned several seats in the 1976 elections. Except for Manifesto, whose founders still publish the eponymous daily, within a few years all these groups and parties dissolved as independent entities. Some leaders and members went underground to join the armed organizations, a few were incarcerated for alleged crimes, and the rest joined left-wing parliamentary groups, such as the Communist, Radical, or, later on, Green Parties.

4. Mirafiori is the name of a suburb of Turin, location of a large FIAT manufactory and the site in this period for heated left-wing labor organization and agitation. The statement's title implicitly proposes a connection between the Student Movement (symbolized by Woodstock) and the working class.

5. *Bandiera rossa* [Red Banner or Red Flag] is a popular communist anthem. The lyrics were written in 1908 by Carlo Tuzzi, the melody borrowed from two folk songs from the region of Lombardy.

6. We used the word "outsider" here to translate the Italian *fuorisede*, which indicates a student who does not reside in the town where he or she studies. While in the United States this is the norm, in Italy it is not, because most students who live in the north or in the center of the country can go to college in their hometown or in nearby cities. Particularly in the 1970s, the "outsiders" were students from the south, where there were just a few colleges. We felt that the word "outsider" expressed the psychological and socio-geographical distance of the *fuorisede* from the local community of students.

7. Giuseppe "Peppino" Impastato (1948–1978) was born in Cinisi, a town near Palermo, Sicily, and the son of a local Mafia chieftain. Refusing to follow his father's model, Impastato became active in radical politics and, in 1976, established the local free radio station Radio Aut. Broadcasts in which Mafia leaders were denounced and satirized were frequent. In 1978, Impastato ran for office in city government. In the run-up to the election, he was murdered by the Badalamenti clan, which had been the subject of his on-air ridicule. In 2001 and 2002 two members of the clan were finally condemned for the crime. Marco Tullio Giordana's film *I cento passi* [*The Hundred Steps*] (2000) is based on Impastato's story.

8. For the use of *Palazzo*, see the introduction (note 9), the translation of the "diary," and the interview with Marco Baliani and Maria Maglietta in this volume.

9. "Colpire al cuore dello stato" [to strike a blow at the heart of the State] had been the slogan of the Red Brigades (BR) and used as an explanation for their strategies and targeted kidnappings.

10. Giorgio Almirante (1914–1988) was the leader of the neo-fascist Movimento Sociale Italiano Destra Nazionale [National Italian Social Movement of the Right, or MSI], the most influential right-wing party of the First Republic (1946–1992). Almirante had been a fascist activist and one of the supporters of the Italian Social Republic in Salò, the puppet-state run by the Nazis to which Mussolini withdrew after the 1943 armistice. Notwithstanding the Italian Constitution's explicit prohibition against the public display of fascist iconography, Almirante's party was inspired by and celebrated fascist ideas, slogans, and symbols. In 1979, he was charged with attempting to revive the Fascist Party. In 1995, the MSI dissolved. Most of its members and leaders devoted their energies to nurturing a new political party, Alleanza Nazionale [National Alliance], led by Gianfranco Fini, former MSI leader and Almirante follower. A few members of the old party formed other new radical groups. In 2008, Alleanza Nazionale, too, dissolved to merge with Silvio Berlusconi's party Forza Italia [Go Italy] into the Popolo della Libertà [People of Freedom]. In 2010, Fini led an internal protest against Berlusconi's oppressive leadership and left the Popolo. Most of the former MSI and Alleanza Nazionale members followed him in the newly founded political movement Futuro e Libertà [Future and Liberty]. Ugo La Malfa (1903–1979), a former partisan and member of the anti-fascist Partito d'Azione [Action Party], participated in the drafting of the Italian Constitution in 1946 and was the leader of the Partito Repubblicano Italiano [Italian Republican Party], a moderately liberal party with great concern for economic and ethical matters. La Malfa's economic politics were particularly innovative and had a great role in Italy's "economic miracle" of the 1950s. After La Malfa's death, his son, Giorgio, led the PRI. The party was almost obliterated after the national judicial investigation into bribery and corruption in Italian political parties known as Mani Pulite [Clean Hands], which began in 1992. Despite their profound differences, in 1978 both Almirante and La Malfa demanded restoring capital punishment, which had been abrogated after the collapse of Mussolini's regime.

11. Giulio Andreotti (1919–), one of the most powerful men in postwar Italy and a lifetime senator since 1991, was a leader of the Christian Democrats, and served repeatedly as prime minister, minister of internal affairs, minister of defense, and minister of foreign affairs between 1972 and 1992, and throughout the period of Aldo Moro's kidnapping and assassination. Nicknamed "Beelzebub" and "Il Divo Giulio," among other epithets, Andreotti was tried unsuccessfully for collusion with the Mafia and other crimes of corruption. He is despised by the Italian Left and legendary for his elusive, sibylline rhetoric and his skill in escaping charges. Andreotti is the subject of Tony Sorrentino's film *Il Divo* (2008).

Francesco Cossiga (1928–2010), another powerful leader of the Christian Democrats and lifetime senator from 1992, succeeded Aldo Moro as minister of internal affairs from 1976 to 1978, and resigned after Moro's assassination. Andreotti and Cossiga were leaders of the "front" within the Italian leadership that refused to negotiate with the BR for Moro's liberation. Cossiga followed Andreotti as prime minister (1979–1980) and became president of the Republic in 1985, serving until 1992. During his presidency, he revealed his participation in the establishment of stay-behind organization Gladio and aroused heated reactions for his destabilizing statements, also known as *picconate* [mattock or pickax blows], about national and international politics.

12. The "Fiera del Levante" is a giant trade fair open to the public, a sort of national state fair visited by hundreds of thousands, that takes place annually in the fall in the southern coastal city of Bari.

13. The term Movimento stands for the Movimento degli studenti [Student Movement], the mass movement that originated in 1968 in schools and universities worldwide. In Italy, the Movimento soon radicalized and gave birth to other extra-parliamentary groups with more specific purposes and ideological nuances.

14. *L'Unità*, founded by Antonio Gramsci in 1924, was the official organ of the Partito Comunista Italiano (PCI) and is now the newspaper of the Partito Democratico (PD), a pro-reform, no longer communist version of the former party. For more on the other two dailies, see note 3.

15. The *carabinieri* are the Italian national police force, similar to France's *gendarmerie*. In distinction to the regular police, which has local jurisdiction, they are a federal entity and constitute a branch of Italy's military.

16. *Sostituto Procuratore* [district attorney] Mario Sossi, considered the nemesis of left-wing terrorists, was kidnapped by the BR in Genoa on April 18, 1974, and held until May 20 of the same year. The BR claimed that their successful kidnapping had achieved their objective of destabilizing state institutions.

17. The author-narrator is referring to the picture of a young left-wing extremist shooting at the police, his face semi-covered by a balaclava, in Via De Amicis, Milan, on May 14, 1977, when policeman Antonio Custra was killed. This photo, taken by an amateur, documents the riots that followed Giorgiana Masi's death (see note 18). It appeared in all the newspapers and soon became one of the most powerful icons of the *anni di piombo*.

18. Francesco Lorusso (1951–1977) was a student and member of Lotta Continua, killed during violent demonstrations in Bologna in March, 1977. A *carabiniere* named Massimo Tramontani—seized by panic—was witnessed repeatedly firing into the crowd of demonstrators, but was absolved during later investigation by application of the Reale Law. Giorgiana Masi (1958–1977), student and member of the Radical Party, was killed by a .22-caliber bullet during a demonstration in Rome on May 12, 1997. A *carabiniere* and another demonstrator were also shot and wounded at the same time. They survived. Despite the existence of films demonstrating the presence at the conflict of armed plainclothes policemen, no public, official investigation has been conducted so far to determine who shot Masi. Only thirty years later has the Italian Parliament considered the creation of a *commissione d'inchiesta* [investigation committee], following a controversial interview with Francesco Cossiga, then minister of the interior, published in *Il Giornale* on October 2008. In the interview, Cossiga advocated the use of armed infiltrators in order to provoke violent reactions and therefore legitimize brutal repression. As an example of this political strategy, he mentioned the tactics he used during the years of lead.

19. On December 12, 1969, a bomb exploded at the headquarters of the Banca Nazionale dell'Agricoltura in Milan's Piazza Fontana. Sixteen people were killed, and eighty-eight were wounded. Three other bombings took place in Rome and Milan on the same day. Police first arrested an anarchist named Giuseppe "Pino" Pinelli, who fell to his death from the fourth floor of Milan's police headquarters during interrogation. Pinelli's death is the basis of Dario Fo's play, *Morte accidentale di un anarchico [Accidental*

Death of an Anarchist], staged for the first time in 1970. National consensus has since established that the bombings were carried out by far-right organizations, possibly supported by Italian secret services and the CIA, in pursuance of the so-called strategy of tension aimed at fomenting a state of emergency. See also the introduction, where these events are discussed in detail.

On May 28, 1874, in the northern industrial city of Brescia, a bomb concealed in a garbage container exploded during a leftist demonstration in the city's Piazza della Loggia, killing eight and wounding over ninety. Again, far-right terrorist groups were suspected of operating in collusion with government secret services. As with Piazza Fontana, most charges against suspected neo-fascist bombers have proved indemonstrable, with the few guilty sentences handed down reversed on appeal.

20. The P38 gesture, named for the famous German pistol, the Walther P38, consisted of the familiar childhood hand gesture of shooting a gun: index finger extended, thumb upraised, other fingers curled into the palm. The P38 gesture with the hand in vertical position became a particular symbol of the extra-parliamentary Italian Left faction known generally as Autonomia, for whom the P38 gesture signified a willingness to shoot, and so represented an escalation beyond the militant raised fist gesture. Please see the performance photograph in this volume.

21. "Stakhanovite" is a term adapted from Stalinist Russia, where a coalminer named Alexey Grigoryevich Stakhanov became a national hero in 1935 for having mined fourteen times his quota of coal. The term is used to describe any indefatigable worker. Count Santorre di Santa Rosa (1783–1825) was an Italian patriot during the early years of the *Risorgimento*, who led an insurrection that briefly established a constitutional government in Piedmont before his betrayal by the Savoy rulers. Exiled first to Paris and then to London, Santa Rosa was killed in 1825 in Greece, having adopted that nation's cause against the Turks. His name is here cited as an example of overheated, self-destructive patriotic heroism.

22. Poet, novelist, and translator Cesare Pavese (1908–1950) published the first Italian translation of Herman Melville's *Moby Dick* in 1941, during a period when modernist American literature exerted a profound influence on a rising generation of anti-fascist artists and intellectuals.

23. The issue of negotiation was particularly controversial. Newly elected Prime Minister Andreotti and his close supporters as well as the communists, the neo-fascists, and the republicans were particularly tight in their opposition against any form of negotiation with the BR, and adopted a monolithic *linea della fermezza* [policy of non-negotiation]. Some Christian Democrats, such as Benigno Zaccagnini (see note 32) and Amintore Fanfani, remained hesitant, however, and elaborated the ambivalent concept of *fermezza flessibile* [flexible policy of negotiation], which, in their views, did not exclude partial contact with the BR. The Partito Socialista and the Partito Radicale declared a pro-negotiation stance, claiming that human life had to take precedence over any political considerations. The left-wing extra-parliamentary groups tried to maintain—albeit with difficulty—a position of equidistance between the State and the BR, but were vocally in favor of negotiation.

24. The sentence "né con le Brigate Rosse né con lo Stato" [neither with the BR nor with the State] appeared in *Lotta Continua* on March 18, 1978, and soon became a slogan of the extra-parliamentary groups.

25. This assertion is not completely true. Some Christian Democrats, in fact, were uncertain about the negotiation issue and maintained an ambiguous double position, favoring negotiation in private yet disavowing it publicly. Albeit in a confused manner, the DC believed it was possible to negotiate for Moro's life without assigning a political status to the BR (see note 23).

26. The narrator is here referring to the novel *Uno, nessuno e centomila* [*One, No one, One Hundred Thousand*] (1927) by Sicilian novelist, short story author, and dramatist Luigi Pirandello (1867–1936). Throughout his oeuvre, Pirandello explored philosophical and existential issues, such as the fragmentation and multiplicity of human identity, the relativity of truth, and the intersections between the notions of madness and normality. He also questioned the conventional elements of genres, particularly of theater. In *Uno, nessuno e centomila*, his last and most philosophical novel, the protagonist Vitangelo "Gegè" Moscarda realizes, almost by chance and for trivial reasons, that all the people around him have different, subjective perceptions of him and that these different personae, or masks, do not coincide with his self-representation. He then seeks his true self, but without success. His conclusion is that the self is unstable and illusory. Leonardo Sciascia also establishes an explicit relationship between Moro and Pirandello in *The Moro Affair*.

27. The joke is homophonic, relying on the southern Italian pronunciation of Aldo as *alto* [tall] and on the word *moro*, which means brunette.

28. A clandestine hideout is referred to as a *covo*, which derives from *covare*, the verb used to describe hens keeping the eggs in the nest warm so they will hatch.

29. During Moro's captivity, on at least two occasions the police received information about apartment eleven in Via Gradoli, where Red Brigadist Mario Moretti lived: once from neighbors, who reported hearing someone use Morse code at night; another time in an obscure circumstance involving a group of Bologna University professors with Romano Prodi, who, years later, served as Italy's prime minister and EU chairman. The first time, the police visited the building and knocked on the door of Moretti's apartment, but left after no one answered. The second time, Prodi reported to the Ministry of the Interior Cossiga that, during a séance, the name "Gradoli" had come out. Cossiga was aware that the indication probably arrived from radical circles close to the Red Brigades and ordered a police search, sent not to Via Gradoli, however, but to a village outside Rome named Gradoli. On April 18, the police finally discovered Moretti's hideout: someone with keys to the apartment had left the water on in the bathroom, and the ensuing flood had forced neighbors to call the fire department. Former Senator Sergio Flamigni is the author of several books that helped set in motion complex conspiracy theories. See *La tela del ragno: Il delitto Moro* (Milan: Kaos, 2003) and *Convergenze parallele: Le Brigate Rosse, i servizi segreti e il delitto Moro* (Milan: Kaos, 1998). Today, the conspiracy theories on the Moro Affair are under discussion. For an ample report on this topic, see Roberto Bartali, "The Red Brigades and the Moro Kidnaping: Secrets and Lies," in *Speaking Out and Silencing: Culture, Society, and Politics in Italy in the 1970s*, edited by Anna Cento Bull and Adalgisa Giorgio (Oxford: Legenda, 2006).

30. Indro Montanelli (1909–2001) was a noted conservative Italian journalist. After writing for several newspapers in Italy and abroad he began his lifetime collaboration with the Milan daily *Corriere della sera* in 1938. Montanelli founded *Il Giornale* in

1973, serving as director until Silvio Berlusconi, the owner, entered politics. In order to free himself from Berlusconi's political pressure, Montanelli resigned from *Il Giornale* and founded *La Voce*. The new paper survived only one year and Montanelli ended his career as the chief letters editor at the *Corriere della sera*, where he answered a letter a day in the column *La stanza di Montanelli* [*Montanelli's Room*]. Montanelli was known for the frank, brisk expression of his political views. During the fascist regime, he openly opposed Mussolini's positions, for which he received a death sentence. During the *anni di piombo*, he opposed Moro's politics of openness toward the Left, and his judgment on Moro was even more severe during the sequester. He was very harsh with the left-wing extremists and, as a result, was shot in both legs by the BR in Milan. Despite his anti-communist and conservative political views, he publicly contested Berlusconi too, denouncing his maneuvers to limit journalistic freedom of expression and his use of authoritarian, fascist-like means to seize the nation.

31. Benigno Zaccagnini (1912–1989) was party secretary of the Christian Democrats as well as one of Moro's closest friends.

32. *Prezzemolina* [*Little Miss Parsley*] is the protagonist of a Tuscan fairy tale included in Italo Calvino's collection of popular *Fiabe italiane* [*Italian Folktales*] (1956). The character of *Prezzemolina* is very similar to the German *Rapunzel*, popularized by the Grimm Brothers.

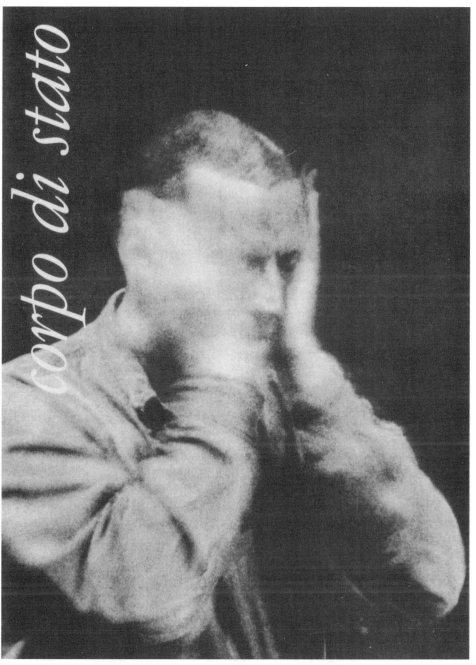

Program distributed at live broadcast of *Corpo di Stato* on RAI 2, May 1998
(© 2003 RCS Libri SpA—Milano)

Rome 1975
(© 2003 RCS Libri SpA—Milano)

Milan 1975
(© 2003 RCS Libri SpA—Milano)

Rome 1977
(© 2003 RCS Libri SpA—Milano)

Milan 1977
(© 2003 RCS Libri SpA—Milano)

Milan 1978
(© 2003 RCS Libri SpA—Milano)

Milan 1978
(© 2003 RCS Libri SpA—Milano)

Milan 1978
(© 2003 RCS Libri SpA—Milano)

CHAPTER 3

Diary

Marco Baliani

Polynieces's body is mixed in with the others, but a few signs of his fallen majesty remain: a sash, a cuff that the victors' scavenging has not dared to profane. He's been dragged there, in the dust, his dripping hair caked with dirt. His corpse, seen like this, in a pile from a distance, looks like a wan puppet surrounded by a boneyard of broken-down scarecrows. It's terrible how, by now, when I try to think about something similar, the powerful image of bodies tossed around like garbage in the Nazi concentration camps comes rushing out at me, the legacy of this century on its way out. Only his sister, Antigone, is able to isolate this body, she sniffs it out, drawn like a magnet to the very place she shouldn't go. By Creon's order, it is impossible and forbidden to bury that body.

Antigone has already defied those orders, she has scattered a handful of dust on that scandalous body, just enough to break the laws of the State so she may follow those that are sacred and her own.

She was discovered by the guards and taken before Creon, but in my imagination I need to see all three of them together, not Antigone before Creon in the Palazzo [palace], but Creon before her, there among the bodies and, among them, on the ground, that illustrious corpse not to be buried.[1]

Felice Cappa was the promoter for the entire project. He was the one to pitch a risky live broadcast for RAI 2 to Carlo Freccero, and he followed the entire creative process of the project, offering suggestions and advice.[2]

I was immediately convinced by the title Felice had suggested: *Corpo di Stato*. There was something in it that rang out, the idea of a corpse at the mercy of the State, but also a play on words between *corpo* and *colpo* of the State.[3]

Going forward from there, little by little, we would discover that it was that body, Moro the man, that was the tap for the stories, turning it let them flow.

For a week I went around repeating that title in my head, waiting for something to flower, waiting for that body to start talking to me. That ancient scene, Antigone and her brother's unburied body, was the first image that came to me. It had visited me many times throughout the course of my lifetime of theatrical wandering. Now she had returned, but under a different sign, in the way of myths always to reveal new essences, hidden spirits.

In 1991 I had directed a cast of one hundred in a ceremony commemorating the August 2, 1980, massacre at the Bologna train station.[4] It was titled *Antigone of the Cities.*

In the middle of Piazza Maggiore we had piled up an enormous mound of dirt. Slightly before the last scene, one hundred bodies danced frenetically without music, embracing and drawing away, and then lying lifeless, abandoned on that burial mound.

Antigone was played by an elderly actress, Rosetta, whom I knew and had already worked with in Alexandria on a choral project about collective memory. She was an amateur actress, a former employee of Borsalino, with a tremendous gift for performance.

She made her way across the mound of earth heaped with corpses, supported by a cane because she had twisted an ankle during rehearsal. She had a long speech, a funerary song for all those unburied dead, victims of the massacres, Polyneices multiplied.

I was following the scene in complete silence from the director's booth, a terrace fronting the piazza. As that limping old woman crossed the world, the crowd of spectators—there were more than ten thousand people watching—held their breath, like me.

My heart raced as I followed her, we hadn't had much time for rehearsal, and the microphone she was wearing was dicey—it had already slipped twice before the start of the show—she wasn't used to wearing it and it was possible the scene wouldn't come off. There would be no other performances, it was one, unrepeatable event. Rosetta came to the end of her piece and suspense was very high in the piazza. It was like a hurricane, I've never heard such applause since.

I don't know what shape theater took in ancient Greece, there are many legends and we all imagine it the way we want to. But that night I felt that we weren't far away from what it must have been like. An entire city there to hear its story told and with the city itself that had commissioned it. They had asked me, an artist, to stage a memory. So that it would not be forgotten.

Now public television with Carlo Freccero was doing something similar. After all there was a *polis* here, too, a public entity that had asked me to tell a story of memory. But this time the jump back in time was short, to our recent past, only twenty years earlier. There weren't one hundred actors, it was just me and the piazza television made for me was much bigger than the one in Bologna.

April 27

I'm with Maria Maglietta and Felice Cappa doing a locations check of the ruins in Traiano's Forum in Rome. Finally they agreed to let us use it. They'd never allowed that before, as we were told by a young conscientious objector whose alternative service was to guard the monuments in the Forum. Just the year before another director had asked for use of the same space and they hadn't allowed it.

We learned later he was talking about Peter Stein.

The supervisor from the Ministry of Cultural Affairs came with us, imploring us with a sort of defeated look on her face—this was her kingdom, after all, and we were invading it—to be mindful of the areas not to be walked on, which ruins to leave alone, and so forth.[5] Above all, she is nervous about the TV equipment, which the techs, slyly, say doesn't weigh that much. She begs us not to have more than fifty spectators, no exceptions will be made—the day of the broadcast there will be more than two hundred people there—and while Felice reassures her I am already imagining how I'll get up on that capital, and how I'll use the other one as a seat during a more intimate part of the story. The grass is long, wild. They'll cut it, she assures us, but I almost like it better this way. You walk on it and your shoes get wet in this, the place of Rome's special humidity.

Curious passersby watch us from the passageway over the Forum. They look at us, think maybe we're shooting a film. A lot of spectators will watch from there on the evening of May 9. Felice considers a gigantic screen that you could see from up there, but then we find out it costs too much and let the idea go.

Maria wanders around, skeptically shaking her head. She's never been fully convinced of doing a live broadcast here. She thinks the setting is too grand and that we run the risk of coming off too "rhetorical": the heart of the State, the heart of Rome, ancient and contemporary, too much taken for granted. But Felice insists, he says we need to be more blasé, that we shouldn't be scared of the commonplace, that television isn't the theater.

We already gave up on the idea of using a big staircase anyway. Maria convinced us, saying I need to stand in the midst of the ruins, at the same height as the audience, without any raised levels, like talking from the ruins, among the pieces of a world that no longer exists, and the fragments will be part and parcel of my narration.

Behind me is a wall of broken tufo, to my left the columns of a temple that, we discover ironically, was a temple of justice. Above the wall behind me you sense there's another city: the theme of the two cities, one visible and the other hidden, will be the center of my story.

I try to rehearse a few of the pieces I've already committed to memory, but it's tough, my gaze is drawn everywhere, I feel lost and alone, the space seems huge and it's not like it's just any place, only two thousand years ago where I am standing now there were people who met, talked, lived. Did they also tell stories of mysterious deaths and horrible years?

I've got Sciascia's *The Moro Affair* in my pocket.[6] I'm rereading the same section, a pitiless and at the same time compassionate description of Moro. It could be a finale, or even a beginning, an introduction, and I'd like to read it with the book in my hand, maybe with my back to the audience, in the grand piazza with the broken columns before me even now, creating a sense of distance:

"And in the end, there, there's the word that for the first time he writes with atrocious nakedness: the word that is finally revealed in its true, profound, and putrid meaning: the word power." "I do not want around me—let me repeat—powerful men." But in the previous letter he had spoken about the authority of the State and party members: it's only now that I have arrived at the awful truth of the word.

He had lived for power and in power until 9 a.m. on that March 16. He had hoped to have power again: maybe to come back and assume it in full, certainly to avoid having to deal with *that* death. But now he knows that others have the power: he sees it in the stupid, ugly, ferocious faces of others. In his *friends*, in his most *faithful companions of happy hours*: the macabre, obscene happy hours of power. *The happy hours*, the happy hours of power. With irony. An irony that came from a distance, now bitter and painful. It doesn't seem that he was ever happy in power. He loved it, but it also caused him suffering. Perhaps being the best of the lot, and the disdain he felt toward all the others, had granted him a certain Christian awareness of his own wretchedness. This awareness was the difference between him and the *others* and the reason why, among all of them—and in a certain sense, *by* all of them—he was the one chosen to die.

The idea of using this piece had remained entrenched until a few days before the opening and then, all of a sudden, without saying anything to each other, almost as one we felt it just didn't work, that it was in the way. It meant opening up another avenue and another vision that I wasn't going to be able to go into in depth. We couldn't let ourselves get sucker-punched by the political personality of Moro, the drama of plots and intrigues that he had taken to his death. No, that way we could have easily fallen into conspiracy theories and conjecture. No, Moro's body was the I-beam of my story, the physicality of his body become burdensome, both alive, as a prisoner, and dead, as a sacrificial victim.

And thus took shape for me another image contained in the title, one where Moro's body flanked Polyneices's unburied body: a tracking shot of frozen faces, people on their feet, contrite, a few actually distraught. Look at them, the men in the Palazzo officiate a funeral rite, the camera scans over them as though mustered in a military parade, they look ahead or down at the floor because there's no coffin where their eyes may come to rest. Aldo Moro's body is not there. It's not there. The actual funeral is taking place elsewhere within the tight-knit family circle. It is a body withdrawn from public view, a body without a State.

It's not far from there to Creon's State, where Polyneices's cumbersome body may not be buried. It's not far from there to the Italian State of non-negotiation that would like in whatever way possible to bury and commemorate Aldo Moro's cumbersome body.[7]

With the withdrawal from public view, that body became an even greater sign of an injustice that has been done, the terminal parabola of an imprisonment that has gone on for too long.

From the beginning, the Moro affair struck me as tragedy. The deeper I waded into documents, the transcripts from various trials, the terrorists' autobiographies, the endless pile of newspaper articles, the closer I came to falling into that tangle I had almost stumbled into any number of times, the more clearly a tragic scene emerged.

How strange: I had before me an observant Christian and yet my secular gaze as a non-Christian didn't see Redemption so much as Destiny.

The concept of actual Christian redemption cannot help but oppose a tragic conscience. The individual always has the chance to save himself and this destroys the tragic feeling of a ruin from which there is no escape. And yet, in Moro's story, everything tipped toward ruin from the beginning, not only that of his physical, material body but that of the world that surrounded him. And this included me, too, and my generation, as if Moro's body dragged an entire historical period behind it, stripping it bare, revealing its relations and contradictions.

At bottom, thinking of the changes that had happened after his death, that death almost brought a sense of catharsis. An era ends, it strips itself of the words that have held it together, and in this, in the path that leads to this, there is always present a kind of inevitability.

I'd like to be able to see the death of Moro as the slaughter of a scapegoat, with him as a necessary sacrificial victim who broke a world apart and put it back together again. But I would like to say it with simple words; the whole text needs to flow like a story. No explanations; just events. You need to feel the presence of the tragic with just a few, very dense images, maybe just a gesture. I imagine lengthening the moments before his death inside that garage, as if we were just on the other side, as if on some ancient altar. At the same time, the rite is brutal, with no sacrality, unavoidable even though it could have been avoided.

The sun has peeked out again from behind the clouds that had gathered, and the air has cleared, sparkling.

I've been away from Rome for more than six years, I spent more than thirty here—almost my whole life—and now I'm back on this subterranean level, in the secret heart of the city, a bit on the sly. During rehearsals I haven't done anything except to move from my hotel in Via Cavour, a few steps away, to come hide myself among the ruins. I'm more Roman than anyone I pass on the streets above. Outside of this fixed route I feel lost. Instead, when I settle myself among the capitals, and doggedly repeat my monologues and stories, I'm at peace, I feel almost protected. This place doesn't scare me; I feel as though I make it more mine with each day that passes, like the cats all over this place, the actual owners of the ruins, even if I did see a giant sewer rat dart out from among the ruins yesterday and no cat dared attack it, so there are still other inhabitants and other strata of life I don't know.

In my imagination, I stretch the bits of broken columns toward the sky. I try to complete the supports, even close up the arches. It must have been a magnificent scene: perhaps those ruins may have made a good backdrop against which a tragedy could play out, even if I think the Romans, clever as they were, missed the sense of tragic depth from the very beginning.

I can almost see Caesar's body, just stabbed by Brutus and his men, fall down the stairway behind me. I can see the tyrant's stunned face and see his body slip, publicly exposed. Tragedy needs open, visible spaces. The men from Caesar's own party arm themselves and stab him. They show themselves, they act, they have no need of intermediaries, of secret silences and ever more secret services.

Here, however, in the 1978 that I need to make come to life, with all the pain those memories bring with them, here the tragedy needs to unfold in anonymous telephone booths, squalid garages, apartments, stolen cars. It takes place in coded texts, letters hidden and then displayed at the opportune moment, reverse blackmails, murky words. It takes place in the noise of a city that soldiers on, that counts the dead and is afraid.

And yet, despite these other scenes, it does not cease being a tragedy.

I try to position myself between two fragments of capitals, as if I were caught between two marble walls. It could be an interesting image to film. I smile. I am thinking more about filming than my own performance. My hand trails over the porous marble. In the carved relief I can see a snail trapped in its shell. I think of the craftsmanship that more than two thousand years ago, with careful strikes of a chisel, made these carvings, even though they were going to be twenty meters in the air, almost invisible from below. And yet, what care, what humble practice, what precision, as if the act of sculpting in itself had sense enough to nurture it. There's something to be learned here: to be a pure vehicle for the art one has, let the story pass through me without getting in the way, without showing off. I need to hide technique, make the narration be heard as something everyone knows, say the act just as it is, above and beyond all content of the narrated story, as if it were an inheritance everyone shared. Listening to me, everyone should feel the need to tell the story themselves, or at least to try. The spectator should see the work as something, by all appearances simple, something very common, an act that is recognizable and beloved.

But at the same time, like this carved capital, I need to be efficient, concise, there should not be one excess element, I need to withdraw to the right degree, just as when experience in the kitchen tells you the dish is ready to be tasted.

But for it to come off like this I need time I haven't got. Usually, a story defines itself and takes shape through performance, the repetition and the audience always different.

After more than five hundred performances, *Kohlhaas* is an almost perfect sculpture, it has reached its classical state: the show begins, the lights focus on an empty chair, there's nothing else on stage, I sit down and the story flows from me as if it were no longer mine. I can listen to myself as if from the outside.[8] It is an unexpected joy every time.

But here the relation is up-ended, and I'm preparing a theater piece that will open on TV and, what's more, as a live broadcast. I won't have time for confirmations save for a couple of tech rehearsals to get used to the cameras, to that ant colony of the TV crew at work.

What is to be done, then? Maria says to me, "To be honest, this is the winning tack, to reduce the artificiality, to be direct, to tell only things that we lived, trying to remember who we were with our feelings, slogans, and needs."

We had felt so impotent when we started exploring the Moro Affair last January, trading findings and working with Alessandra Ghiglione, who would fax us drafts of outlines for the content and staging of the piece. The sheer mass of information was too enormous, we felt lost in it, and worse, we ran the risk of just mucking around in all the slime that still submerges the truth of this case.

Then I happened across a short book by Adriano Sofri, *Moro's Shadow*.[9] A different approach, an effort to explore through the Moro Affair the conduct, or, rather, the character of a people, the realm of their emotional life.

In particular, at a certain point Sofri tries to capture a shadowy sensation held in common by the front of public figures who refused to negotiate, and present also, maybe, within the souls of some of the Red Brigades themselves, a mixture of self-pity and pride in the face of the willed sacrifice of a human being. A mixture of vanity and the conviction of having fulfilled one's duty to the last. To track down this sentiment, Sofri uses an autobiographical story of the killing of his sick dog when he was a teenager and consented to the cruel act, and he reflects on the strange, virile pain he felt after it was done, as though he now felt like a grown-up.

But now, years afterward, he asks himself: Why didn't I take action to stop it from happening?

That brief story, a digression in the book, seemed to offer me a unique pathway, effective in its simplicity, to speak in the first person of my own experience, entering that way into a much larger History, illuminating it sharply by a slanting light.

It was Maria who caught me off guard one morning with a simple question we hadn't had the intuition to ask 'til then.

Where had I been during the fifty-five days of Moro's imprisonment? What had I been doing? How did I shift from political struggle to theater? What was taking place inside and around me?

Once these and similar questions had been clearly formulated, for some time I did nothing but remember. I suddenly had the right to talk, rather than letting the newspapers and books do the talking.

The documents, the newspaper cuttings, became the background, History became a tapestry threaded with constellations of smaller stories, episodes, names, friends I'd lost in memory, places in the city.

I began an interior excavation, very painful at times, and every day ended with a revelation, with the discovery of repressed material lying somewhere inside my memory, abandoned.

During those *memory days* I would watch Mirto, my twenty-one-year-old son, as he listened to my stories with the air of someone unexpectedly discovering a new dimension. He had heard little or nothing from me about those years, a few snatches of documentary fact, a couple of remarks, folklore. Now instead he felt he was watching me as I merged into a landscape utterly unknown to him.

I would talk and then write, filling pages and pages in a notebook Maria and Alessandra transcribed daily onto a computer, trying to order them in a progression. Now we felt enthusiasm, we were on the right track, the map was filling up—in fact it was overflowing—we were going to have to choose what to keep and what to cut. But we would say it all, say how we really felt then, not hiding, not reading those events with the wisdom of hindsight, not claiming professorial detachment, but really being there, performing myself of twenty years before.

Only then could I look at those moments, stand face to face with that politician and tie together once again the scattered threads of a process that had unfolded in confusion and disillusionment, a process I could now recount due to the sole fact that I was still here and could tell it.

Only four days 'til the live broadcast. The bright sun bears down and burns off the night's humidity. It's been raining hard the last few days and we had to cancel rehearsals, losing three days of preparation.

The RAI techs are good at their jobs, they're into the project and I often notice them standing there with open mouths during rehearsals as they listen to my stories. Some of them come up to me and tell me about themselves during those years, it all turns into a great coming-and-going of different generations. Everyone adds their own piece, each one wants to tell their own personal episode. It's a good sign, it means the story doesn't exhaust itself in me alone but generates other stories in turn, the best possible outcome for a narrator.

The city workers have cut the grass short all around the ruins where the story will be filmed so the ancient stones will stand out in greater relief.

I watch myself in the monitor they've set up in the grassy area for the first rehearsals: to me I look awkward and heavy, a thick chunk of a man who doesn't correspond to the way I feel inside, as though the passing years have increased the detachment between the image I have of myself and the way I really look.

Seeing myself like that, I perceive the time passed between the me of that time and the storyteller of today. Twenty years, truly strange—in theater we usually don't tell our recent past, it's always too risky, the facts are too close. Plus these twenty years seem three times as long if you consider how much the world around us has changed, it's as though much more time than that has passed, and maybe it really has. Who understands time, anyway?

I watch the video images we'll insert in between my stories, and those faces, the clothes, and the settings really do seem to come from some other era, perhaps even from another country.

Working with Michele Buri, an editing genius I met at RAI when I filmed *Kohlhaas* for TV, we assembled a montage of photos from that era, zooming in to them, moving the camera over them, and mixing them with sounds from the era, pieces of free radio transmissions, songs by Area, news footage, arranging them into fifteen- or twenty-second sequences between one story and another.[10] You see faces, helmets, tire irons, tear gas, police trucks, marches, riots, banners. They arouse incredible emotions and really seem to come from some other, far-off world.

But no, that was us, society was that, that was the violence, those were the signs of the world around us.

So I guess on stage I'll be that person I see in the monitor: a solitary figure telling stories to ghosts—no, fortunately there will be flesh-and-blood spectators. There I'll be, narrating my own story. This too is uncommon. Usually stories are told in the third person so that the narrator can take the necessary distance from the characters he calls forth.

Doubts arise I shouldn't be having at this point, it's too late: is this all too narcissistic?

What if it turns out to be a survivor's tale, like those guys who return from intense experiences or dangerous times, and talk about them but no one listens, or they listen only with annoyance. Maybe people will refuse to dig around again in that era we've all tried to avoid speaking about too much.

Last night in the hotel I reread my beloved Camus: "They sat at a round table, three young men and him, the old one. He recounted his paltry adventures. . . . He left no pauses in the story, hurrying to tell it all before they left. He chose from his own past what he thought would most interest his listeners: being listened to was his only vice . . . at the end of a life, old age comes back up like nausea. It all ends up with not being listened to anymore . . . as for him, he needed them to listen so he could believe in his own life."[11]

What a kick in the stomach! The perfect reading to strengthen my preparation, as though before stepping into the ring a boxer sat down to watch a video of all the knockouts he'd taken.

OK, so what? The risk is worth running and anyway, maybe Camus's old man told stories badly or tried too hard to please his listeners. Or maybe a person only has lousy stories to tell, or can't remember which of his experiences were the necessary, fundamental ones. It's so hard to find an order in the stories you choose to compose your life. We pass right through the middle of life and only later and with much patience can we discern something useful for ourselves and for those we speak to, that is, for those who remain. I always think of storytelling as an extreme, ultimate act, as though after the last story the narrator could drop dead on the spot. If you imagine it that way you can't help telling powerful, necessary stories, it's better to believe that once you're done with the story, you're finished, and only a few phrases will survive you, a few images, a few little tales to hand down.

No, there's nothing I can do now but leap in.

I have very little time to learn to look into the camera, to stick my eyes in there as though I were speaking to someone inside it, but in some passages of the story it's absolutely necessary. I always have to remember that my spectators aren't only the ones sitting in front of me on the stones of the Roman Forum, that most of them are hidden in the ether, inside those little red lights blinking threateningly on the TV cameras. At the same time I'll have an audience of a hundred or so twenty-year-olds like my son, who'll be there in the middle of them, and instinctively—because of my life in theater—I want to look for their eyes, talk directly to them, not to mention the thirty or so other spectators on my left, almost behind me. This is terrible, I'll never turn to speak to them, they're only put there as a background, to give the television audience the impression of a community gathered around the storyteller. I feel like I'm betraying them, they'll have to follow my story from the side without ever meeting my eyes. The techs tell me it'll work just fine; I shake my head but accept it.

With my voice also, with the microphone, I won't need that vocal power you use in the theater, I can benefit from the greater intimacy in moments of reflection; this morning during a sound check the headset mike's battery case flew out of my pocket, I waved to the sound man to change it during a fifteen-second break in the filming, there was suddenly this massive traffic of hands all over my body, I felt like a race car in a pit stop, they were all more agitated than I was, when the time was up I was all ready to go, but if it happens during the live broadcast it'll be a disaster.

I've always distrusted machines and technology, not in a snobbish way, but instinctively I stay away from them, maybe that's why my theater has gradually become so Franciscan, just words and bodies, one or two objects and nothing more.

But here it's different, the tangle of cables, the fixed cameras, the mobile one, the mute signals the technicians exchange among themselves, all this swarming of technology and technicians makes me even more solitary and strange, but that's all right, it's what's needed.

I have changed the names of the friends and other people who appear in my stories. Maria's right about this, we must be respectful. I won't call them by the names I knew them by, but I know that as soon as I start talking about them I'll see them clear as day, a different name won't be able to hide them from the eyes of memory.

We've kept the real name of only one comrade: Peppino Impastato, killed by the Mafia the same day Moro was murdered. We thought about it a lot and finally decided. We'll begin by telling about the two parallel deaths, in dense, fast sequences, cutting from one to the other as though it was all one single event.

Peppino is part of me, not only because I knew and admired him, but because of the choice he made to get his hands dirty, to take action for real with other people, a way of doing political work far from mere revolutionary rhetoric. I already admired him for his way of getting down to work with humility, with the means he had at hand.

And Peppino had been buried in the general oblivion, relegated to silence, sort of like all of us and all those years never spoken of. Now I had the chance to bring him back to life, even if only for the few moments of his assassination.

Brecht said, happy the people who need no heroes. I don't think we're so blessed. No, we desperately need heroic figures, only there aren't any. But Peppino in his way was a hero, so I'm going to tell his story by combining it, scandalously, with Moro's. An unknown body next to a famous one, a silent body flanked by a noisy one.

We just found out that today, one day before the live broadcast, there's going to be a concert rally held by Legambiente about two steps away from here, by the Imperial Fora.[12] A huge mess. Now I have to rehearse while drowned out by loudspeakers blasting at maximum decibels, they even spill into my own microphone, distorting everything. I speak as though mute, the techs listen with their headphones on, the whole thing becomes hallucinatory.

It just demands extra discipline, no different from what I demand of my actors when I direct them. I push forward as best I can.

Late tonight we'll do a taping as though live. That way, if it rains tomorrow, at least we'll have a decent dress rehearsal to broadcast on TV. But I don't want to think about that. It just must not rain, that's all.

The good God of tempests will be distracted tomorrow, there are so many places in the world to make it rain. Does he have to do it right here?

Final preparations, it's 1 a.m., we filmed an excellent rehearsal. They ask me whether I want to review the tape tonight. No, I'd rather not, I'd rather stay with all the good and bad sensations I had running live. In any case I'm completely in their hands now, a hostage to framing, tracking shots, wide angles or whatever. I just have to try to be myself and use all my experience as a narrator. They can worry about the rest.

Not to say that I wouldn't like to stick my nose in their business and give advice. That's a fascinating world, too, I know. When I filmed *Teatro di guerra* with Mario Martone, I was amazed by the set, the camera movement, and even more by the editing, it's a whole separate territory, first they steal life as the actor relives it, then they recompose it according to a poetics and a vision the actor is completely unaware of.[13]

Sooner or later I'd like to give it a try myself, it attracts me. But not today, I don't have time, I have to be ready to go, no distractions, no second thoughts.

These days I feel like an athlete training to break a record or attempt some incredible feat. I watch what I eat, I take care to sleep right, I don't waste energy, I exercise.

Even better, maybe here amid the ruins I can picture myself like an ancient gladiator. That's it, if I mess up, I'll be ripped to shreds by the video audience, they're my adversaries, they challenge my right to be here speaking, ready to cheer if I meet the test but to destroy me if I come up short.

No, I'm being too dramatic, it's not like that at all. The important thing is to remember the golden rule of theater: for the spectator, the event they are witnessing is unique and unrepeatable, there's no such thing as a mistake unless the actor himself draws attention to it in a moment of fear, panic, or inexperience. Other than that, nothing that happens is a mistake. At most there might be a second or two of hovering in the air without a net below, but you can't ever lose your place, because every script is subject to change.

Once, during a performance of my show *Oz*, which I wrote and directed, a halogen lamp exploded on stage, the lights went out and in the darkness of the packed house the fire marshals noticed smoke rising from the lamp's burned wires. With no hesitation they leapt in and ran backstage as the four actors performed a scene in which they were being held prisoner. Not wanting to burst in on the scene underway, the firemen opened their hoses and began spraying the whole stage area with fire-retardant foam.

This all took place in the very moment when the four characters were attempting to unleash a jailhouse revolt against the wizards of Oz who were imprisoning them.

When the lights came back on, the audience saw four bodies covered in white foam, knocked to the ground by the force of the spray and totally confused about what to do.

The scene was perfect. Just like the script demanded, the revolt had been put down.

There was a thunderous, thrilled applause.

Too bad we could never repeat the scene that way. But for the audience that night, that was the way the show was supposed to be.

May 9, 1998

Here we go, the live broadcast is starting in a few minutes, for the last time I'm going over a few of the most difficult passages. I feel strangely calm, moving slowly and not reacting to the excitement of the technicians and the spectators, who know they're going to be in the film, too.

Mirto gives me a thumbs up. I smile back at him. Maria is already seated, she seems calm too.

I look into the eyes of the camera; in a few minutes, in a flash I'll be seen by a vast audience I couldn't reach in ten years of stage performance. But somehow I tremble more when I'm about to go on stage. Here it's different.

I know they're there, the spectators, but I can't hear them. I sense only these ardent young people waiting to hear a story from twenty years ago, when they were just being born, from their parents' era. That's enough for me.

Come on, I'm about to tell a piece of our history, it's worth it, I'll take the risk.

Here we go. The first camera operator is pointing at me, counting down from twenty, fifteen, ten seconds, suddenly I'm totally seized with fear, everything goes foggy, it's all fog.

Then the signal goes off and my body moves forward, it knows what to do, where to look, it has a good memory, this body of mine.

Old Sam Beckett was right. "My body will do its best without me."[14]

Notes

1. Pier Paolo Pasolini first used the word *Palazzo* as a metaphor for hegemonic power. For more on this use, see the introduction (note 9), the translation of *Body of State*, and the interview with Marco Baliani and Maria Maglietta in this volume.

2. RAI 2 is one of Italy's three public television channels.

3. *Corpo* means body, but with the switch of one consonant, "l" for "r," it becomes *colpo*. *Colpo di Stato* in Italian means "coup d'état."

4. This was the date of the bombings at the Bologna train station on August 2, 1980, that were later attributed to right-wing terrorists. Please see the introduction.

5. The Ministry of Cultural Affairs (in Italian, *Beni culturali*) controls access and use of Italy's cultural patrimony, which includes all public museums, archeological sites, and so forth.

6. Leonardo Sciascia (1921–1989), the Sicilian writer, was a member of Parliament representing the Radical Party. He served on the parliamentary commission investigating Moro's death and *L'Affaire Moro* [*The Moro Affair and the Mystery of Majorana*, translated by Sacha Rabinovitch (New York/Manchester, UK: Carcanet, 1987)] was his own minority report.

7. *Fermezza* was the term used to describe the State's refusal to bargain with the Red Brigades for Moro's freedom. See the translation of *Body of State*, note 23.

8. *Kohlhaas* is Baliani's performance piece based on the Heinrich von Kleist novella, published in an 1810 collection, about the wanton display of a ruler's absolute power. Please see the introduction for more information on this and and others of Baliani's works.

9. Adriano Sofri, *L'ombra di Moro* (Palermo: Sellerio, 1991). Adriano Sofri, a former leader of Lotta Continua, is serving a life sentence. He was convicted, with Ovidio Bompressi and Giorgio Pietrostefani, of the murder of Luigi Calabresi, the police official in charge of the investigation of the 1969 bombing in Milan's Piazza Fontana. For more on Piazza Fontana and for a review of some of the political coalitions, see the introduction.

10. "Free radio" is *radio libera*. In 1976, Italy liberalized broadcast regulations such that it became possible for individuals and small groups to establish radio stations independent of the government-run RAI. Especially in the later 1970s, these stations often became a means of social and political communication for young people and the leftist youth movement.

11. Albert Camus, *Between Hell and Reason: Essays from the Resistance Newspaper Combat, 1944–1947*, edited and translated by Alexandre de Gramont (Middletown, CT: Wesleyan University Press, 1991).

12. Legambiente is an environmental activist group.

13. Mario Martone, the Neapolitan filmmaker and theater director, was born in 1959. The film *Teatro di guerra* (*Theater of War*, 1998) tells the story of a Neapolitan theater company that plans to travel to Sarajevo to stage a production of Aeschylus's *Seven Against Thebes*.

14. The citation is from Samuel Beckett's "From an Abandoned Work," dated 1954–1955 in Samuel Beckett, *The Complete Short Prose, 1929–1989* (New York: Grove Press, 1995), 155–64. In a personal communication, Baliani explains that the final words of "From an Abandoned Work" are "My body doing its best without me" (in the Italian translation Baliani read, "Il mio corpo faceva del suo meglio senza di me"), but that he had remembered the verb in the future tense.

CHAPTER 4

Interview with Marco Baliani and Maria Maglietta, April 19, 2009

Nicoletta Marini-Maio, Ellen Nerenberg, and Thomas Simpson

This interview took place in a hotel room in New York City, at the end of the 2009 Annual Conference of the American Association for Italian Studies. It expands on the topics discussed in the roundtable titled "Resistere Narrando" [Resisting by Narrating], in which Marco Baliani participated. Most of the interview was conducted with Marco Baliani. The director of Body of State *and Marco Baliani's collaborator and partner, Maria Maglietta, arrived toward the end.*

Q: Is doing theater, and especially *Body of State*, a form of therapy for you?

MB: Theater is always a form of therapy, even when you think it isn't. But what do we mean by therapy? Does therapy presuppose healing? In that case, no, theater does not heal, it forces us always to rework the same. . . . It's not that once you've finished the performance, that conflict is resolved. Theater is like the wound of Philoctetes, an open wound, every night you stick the knife in the same wound. It's therapeutic in the sense that it forces you to talk about the wound; even in comic theater there's always a wound. I think theater is about wounds, scars, spiritual wounds, wounds of character, conflicts. But usually by therapy we mean a process in which, whether by talking or through expressive action, a problem is solved. I don't believe that theater heals. Otherwise everyone would do it.

Q: Let's go back to the idea of Greek theater. It must be cathartic; there must be a catharsis for the audience, not for the performer.

MB: It's different for the actor than for the audience. I have never understood this thing about catharsis very well, because we've taken it to mean that once the performance is over, we're liberated from the problem. I'm not sure that's what the Greeks meant by the word "catharsis." In my opinion, the word "catharsis" means making the problem visible for the community. It isn't setting aside the conflict, as though having shown it on stage somehow removes it as a social problem for the community. It's just the contrary. In my opinion, thanks to the fact that the conflict has been demonstrated, the community has the right and the opportunity to discuss it. This fact is cathartic, the fact that the conflict has become patrimony of the community. I don't know about the etymology, but it doesn't sound to me like something that, once you've done it, both audience and actor go away relieved, as though they've released their tensions. I don't think anything has been solved. After you've seen Iphigenia and Agamemnon, what have you solved? It isn't that once the performance is over, the tragedy has come to an end. True, the sun set, the audience went home, but that theme went on working in their consciences. I imagine they went home very uneasy, not pacified. If by catharsis you mean to be left refreshed, serene, I don't think so. . . . They went home uneasy, but finally someone had spoken about that problem, therefore it was therapeutically very important for the community; that is, they'd had the courage to talk about the fact that power, the craving for power, can get to the point where a father will deny that his own daughter belongs to him. Thus it was a matter that concerned everyone, in their everyday lives, and that concerns us today as well.

Q: You say that the repetition of this therapeutic, community action does not lead to healing. Freud on the other hand says that the constant re-elaboration of grief will ultimately lead to healing; the object is introjected and overcome. But you don't think your theater will finally lead to . . .

MB: No, for me, no . . .

Q: You'll never arrive at the moment of . . .

MB: For me, there's no healing, and every time I repeat it, I feel worse.

Q: But what about the polis? Because you said you are addressing the polis, you say so in your "Diary," you say that in *Body of State* you take inspiration from Greek theater and you address the polis. Shouldn't the polis sooner or later be healed? Won't it elaborate its grief and finally overcome it?

MB: But to overcome that grief, speaking of Moro, the State would have to tell us who ordered the killing. It isn't up to theater to overcome this social conflict; you can only overcome it politically. Speaking to the polis, theater gives the polis the right to say that it's a problem, to say that it's a conflict. But I don't think it can resolve that conflict, it isn't theater's responsibility to resolve it; otherwise it would become juridical, sociological, educational. That is, theater has the responsibility to speak, to intensify that conflict, turning it into an excellent testing ground for the community. Then the community has to demand of politics, of those who govern the community, to take steps to bring an end to the conflict. We'll be healed of the Moro problem when they tell us who fired the bullets, who was working for the secret services; because the room in Via Gradoli was inhabited by terrorists, by the Red Brigades (BR), but someone had rented that apartment. . . .

Q: But that's not the central conflict you talk about in *Body of State*.

MB: No, it's not. The central conflict is violence. It's a problem without an answer. There is no social model in which that problem is resolved. That is, there is no social model that can say, "Now justice is working." There's no society in which justice functions perfectly. Those who have tried to make perfect justice have produced terror.

Q: Other than the idea of justice, isn't the concept of memory also important? With your work you contribute to constructing a memory of the event; you construct it, reconstruct it in some way. You give a kind of legitimacy to the encounter between your biographical memory and collective memory.

MB: That's right.

Q: Thus you help the polis to think of this event in a new, different way, because it's been filtered by your biographical experience and your subjective memory.

MB: Yes, that's true. I think that is the responsibility of art. Not that I'm special. That is, when Picasso paints "Guernica," he's doing the same thing, that is, as you said yesterday, art is the permission to pull an element, a subject, a small fragment, out of the confused tangle of history, and put it into relief artistically, with a particular language. . . . The content on its own is not sufficient. This is an important theme for me, which is little discussed: we always talk about the content, but it's the form through which the content is communicated that produces, or fails to produce, what we're talking about. Not the content itself.

Q: You talk about the importance of the effect of the performance in creating community in a certain sense. At the same time, you say that the content of the actor's discourse is less important than people think. So, as an actor on stage, what is your role with regard to the audience? If it isn't the content you provide that creates the community, what is it that the actor does on stage that arouses this sense of community?

MB: No, I don't mean to say that the content isn't important, absolutely not, because if you don't have a content to be communicated urgently . . . I mean, a good technical actor can bring anything on stage and make it work, especially if the actor has some charisma, some talent, if he's done some television. An actor who's done some television can go on stage and read the yellow pages, but that's beside the point, that's not the content we're talking about. The fundamental content is the poetic content, the reason why the actor or group of actors stages that material. That is intimately interrelated with the form. It's not that the content by itself is not important; rather, it's not sufficient, it's not enough to determine the outcome of shared communication with the polis. There has to be a form, and that form determines whether the content is put into relief or obscured.

Q: Okay, therefore people respond to *Body of State* by saying, "I remember that, it happened to me, I recognize myself in this, I identify myself in this. . . ." And so community is created. This can be found not only in those who lived through the 1970s in Italy and those who have read about the era and have come to understand something about it, but also, for example, American students who have taken a course on the Holocaust, and who therefore have confronted certain problems, certain very important issues and questions, they too identify with the ethical doubt you embody on stage. Is it the actor, or what is it concretely, in the form of *Body of State*, that creates this possibility on the part of the audience?

MB: I think they're triggered by something quite unusual, because usually in theater the actor doesn't recount himself, usually the actor interprets a character, or when he does recount, he recounts distant events, even stories centuries old, which do not affect him directly. True, they always affect him, but there's a transliteration, the actor puts on a mask, and thanks to that mask the actor can say a whole series of things that he might not be able to say without the mask. So the *Body of State* performance is very unusual and I wouldn't set it as a model. You can't always have a narrating "I," taking up historical events in the first person, who manages to clarify or complicate them like *Body of State*. So we're talking about a very unusual form here, triggered by the very first words of the text. These words permit spectators to understand that we are entering into a biography, so if I had to define *Body of State*, I'd call it biographical theater; we're speaking of biography because it begins with "I was twenty-eight, a father for a year, and I'd been doing theater for four years." This triggers a reaction in the spectators, who think, "Ah, this isn't a comedy, it isn't a tragedy, and it's not a 'Once upon a time'–type story." In the first ten minutes of a play, you establish the conventions through which the spectators will read it. You establish the language itself, as though you were saying, "My play, my poetics, are these." You have to make the spectator understand this in the first ten minutes, so the viewer can decide whether to go along or not. I'm sitting glued to a chair and it's obvious that I'm not going to get up. After ten minutes the spectators understand that I'm not going to get up from that chair. That's a convention. In *Body of State*, the convention is that narrating "I." I think that's what triggers the process of identification, that pulsating, extremely sincere "I," very real, very moved. Don't you think? Forget about the truth, or reality. It's in those first words, with all the presence of all the years that have since passed. When I say, "I was twenty-eight," what I'm saying above all is, "I'm still alive," I'm here to recount these things with the authority of the thirty years that have gone by, thirty years really gone by, so there's . . .

Q: Is it in a certain sense like Dante?

MB: Yes, "In the middle of the journey of our life . . ."

Q: "I found myself astray in a dark wood . . ." It witnesses the fact that he is listening and that he has survived. But speaking of these thirty years that have passed, you say that the speaker in *Body of State* is unique because in other works you interpret a character. But isn't it also true that the narrating "I," that twenty-eight-year-old, is also a character you are performing?

MB: Sure, that's true too. Through the language of theater I have to make it so that when I'm at the demonstration in '71, I'm the Marco Baliani of '71, but there's always a premise. From a Brechtian viewpoint, the spectator knows that the narrator is speaking thirty years later, because at the beginning someone said, "Once upon a time Marco Baliani was twenty-eight in 1978." From there, the spectator accepts that you're recounting that on March 21 you were there in the car with Maria. The spectator accepts, as in all theatrical convention, when someone sets up at the beginning, saying "To be or not to be," the spectator accepts that it's Hamlet speaking, because the actor has the formal, aesthetic, linguistic authority to establish that particular convention. I'll give you an example: *Body of State* was a finalist for a literary prize, the Volponi Award. There were various books in competition, and they assigned an actor to read the first pages of *Body of State*, and they chose an actor from the traditional theater. I was there, and I realized immediately that . . . it was terrible, terrible! "Valle Giulia, School of Architecture, 1973." Argh! You understand immediately what a catastrophe it would have been if Gassman had performed it, after two pages you would have fled from the theater, it was unbearable.[1]

Q: So there was an ethical inspiration.

MB: Which is why it's still more that it's really how you do it that allows the text to pulsate or not. The text in itself is important; we're really talking specifically about 1978. But it's a disaster if you do it bombastically or dripping with pathos. This is something I learned through the process of constructing the play, with Maria watching. There's all the work of the actor behind it to arrive at the form it finally takes. The apparent simplicity that seems almost a bit cold, perhaps not cold exactly, but not dripping with emotion. Sure, in certain moments I am moved despite myself, because I'm speaking of things that concern me intimately. But I do it in a way so as not to descend into, to not empathize to the point that . . .

Q: This principle of apparent simplicity is very neoclassical.

MB: Apparent simplicity.

Q: Very interesting. But the central conflict in *Body of State*, if we remove it from its context and take it symbolically, is the same central conflict as *Kohlhaas*.[2]

MB: Yes.

Q: So what is the difference between these two types of theater, between these two characters and the way of recounting them?

MB: *Kohlhaas* is a horseback ride, I don't know any other way to describe it. It's a story in which the narrating body comes forward as the principal dimension of the work, so that linguistically, *Kohlhaas* is a corporeal language, while in *Body of State*, even though it's all about bodies, my own body is very still. It's much more contained and there are images that break up the possibility of empathizing too much with what is being said. The images are actual breathing stops, stops that compel the spectator to enter into a language that has nothing to do with theater, familiar images from the media that amplify the awareness that we're speaking of those years, images of . . .

Q: Of the polis.

MB: Of the polis. This is the discourse of truth: the photos are the truth. Of course that's not really so, because they're photos, someone moved the camera in a particular way to emphasize something, or worked in some way with the language of photography. But in *Kohlhaas*, from the very start it's one long horseback ride, it's the art of storytelling in its pure state, like Benjamin said, it's all there, there's the council . . .

Q: But there's no longer the filter of the actor playing himself. In *Body of State* there's a body, yours, that is performing another body . . .

MB: Me thirty years ago . . .

Q: You who are absent and present at the same time. It's much more Brechtian, I think.

MB: I think so, too.

Q: But *Kohlhaas* excludes that filter or pretends it's not there.

MB: In *Kohlhaas* I play twenty different characters, I act them, which means I cannot be any of the twenty. The audience understands this from the beginning when I say, "Many years ago in the land of Germany there lived a man named Michael Kohlhaas." It's like saying, "Once upon a time . . ."

Q: And there ends the Brechtian intervention.

MB: No, there are other moments when it returns: there's a moment when I interrupt the story and speak directly to the spectators, saying, "You tell me, if a man can do this, then how can justice exist?" and I stop there to wait for someone to answer.

Q: Has anyone ever answered?

MB: Twice. They both said, "No, it doesn't." Both times in Sicily.

[laughter]

Q: How did American audiences feel different to you from Italian audiences during the performance?

MB: I felt more of an effort to understand, whereas the Italian public goes more on emotion. But remember that we're comparing two different plays that can't be compared, because the rhythm of the American version is tied to the presence of subtitles. It's no small matter; in America there was never really a theatrical setting, except the one time when we had theater lighting, which makes a big difference. In Italy when I sit down to do Moro, the lights go out, you hear the song, and when the lights go back on, bang! there's a violent side light from the right; it's the garage. When I do Peppino, that light goes out and the sunlight comes from the left, bang! the hot light, bang! the cold light, which is a kind of language. It creates a very different theatrical mix. By contrast, here in America, it was still more Brechtian [laughs], we made it more intellectual, if you like, in the positive sense of the term, in that the tempo of the subtitles made people need to understand what I was talking about, to understand more than to feel. In Italy I don't need to make people understand, because we're talking about something that more or less everyone knows about. When I perform it in high schools or for young people, I also slow down the rhythms, because I realize they need to understand what I'm talking about, who I'm talking about. I can presume a greater level of knowledge when I perform in the evening than when I perform in the schools. . . . I also make cuts on the fly when I see it's useless to mention things they know nothing about, for example it's useless for me to say, "He was president of the Christian Democrats. . . ." When I talk about Moro for evening audiences, I stretch out the part about Moro a bit because the audience knows who he was. A high school student has no idea who Moro was, so I cut it down. How you use language is always a problem, how you use language renders the communication of one type or another. So to answer your question, here I felt the audience's need to understand, which I was glad of, because it's another form of . . .

Q: Your presence continues on stage, that is, you don't disappear from the story, which is interesting because you said that the images . . . I wanted to ask you about the relationship between the narrator, you on stage, and the projected images you present, because someone in our audience suggested that the images substituted the chorus of Greek theater.

MB: Beautiful!

Q: Yes, beautiful. It was a student. So I wanted to ask about your relationship to that material, when you are still continuously present. That is, you don't disappear.

MB: When I perform in Italy, I usually watch the images, I don't leave the stage, and when I can do it the way I like to, in the right theaters, my shadow adds itself to the images . . . you see me in silhouette, you see my shape on the screen, I turn my back to the audience and watch what's happening on the screen, so I become like a spectator, then reenter while the images are still running, at the moment when you see the youth with his arm raised. I reenter in that moment and position myself under the raised pistol. I'm a dark shadow below it. There's a language game of relationship with the image. That's the scene of Francesco Lorusso, who's the young man on the stretcher that you see three times. Every time I see that image I turn away because I can't stand to watch it, but not for linguistic reasons; it feels like a blow to the heart. They killed him in Bologna during a demonstration. I cut that out for the American performances because who knows who Francesco Lorusso is?[3] You'd have to explain to people . . .

Q: So here you're less a spectator, you're less part of the chorus in the American version, right?

MB: Yes, yes.

Q: Here, your presentation is more as a mediator of history.

MB: Exactly! I serve as a filter between history and myself, thus the idea never to entirely disappear from the screen.

Q: That's why during the discussions afterward it's been so important to return to the fact that you're an artist, because . . .

MB: That's right, brava!

Q: Your continuous presence on stage tends to provide this mediating presence and you become more an intellectual than an artist. Do you feel that? What's your feeling about this idea of being either intellectual or artist, or rather both characters simultaneously, if we call them that?

MB: First of all, I wouldn't distinguish the two. Why distinguish the intellectual from the artist? An artist can be an intellectual too. Whether or not he wants to, that's the function he's performing, so it's better to be conscious of the fact . . .

Q: Now we're getting into a huge topic—that is, the role of intellectuals in Italian society today . . .

MB: If only they had a role. . . .

[laughter]

MB: In our history the figure of the intellectual has gone through many phases. It's very difficult today to define . . . I think today it's a question of absence, but we'd get into a controversy here. . . .

Q: No no, it's interesting, we have plenty of time!

MB: I think a whole series of roles have come to an end . . . that is, Pasolini had a lot of opinions about intellectuals that no longer work. The intellectual no longer exists the way Pasolini and Sciascia thought of it, in the sense that today . . . I don't think Pasolini and Sciascia would have gone on the talk shows; that's the difference. Before, people said intellectuals must be organic to the class struggle, but today they're organic to the mass media. The intellectual no longer causes scandal; on the contrary, today, intellectuals seek to merchandise scandals; scandals have become a commodity. Ideas are commodities, images are commodities, art has become a commodity, especially painting; it's all in the hands of dealers. In such a situation it's very difficult to carve out the sort of role Pasolini pictured. Pasolini imagined many roles for the intellectual, but it finally came down to something very extreme, an intellectual who recalled the Passion of

Christ—that is, the duty of the intellectual was to sacrifice himself like a martyr. And that's just how Pasolini ended up; in his poetry he anticipated how he was to end up. He carried his disillusionment to its ultimate consequences. Before that, he had believed an intellectual's testimony was to give witness. But he saw it wasn't working. . . . In the *Scritti corsari*, the last pieces he wrote for *Corriere della sera*, he understands perfectly the effect of the arrival of television; he sees it very clearly.[4] In the face of what he sees, he asserts a claim to an extremism that derives from his Catholicism, from his deep roots in the Catholic tradition, that is, the Passion, the idea that the intellectual sacrifices his own body. The body becomes the extreme . . . the erotic body, the sexual body, that body is ultimately the only manifestation that can contest power. That's Pasolini's journey. But even this doesn't work anymore; even this can easily be sold on a talk show.

Q: Right, like the television spokesmodels and similar commercialization.

MB: It's very complicated nowadays, you have to be able to refuse to go along with the game.

Q: How can theater represent an alternative?

MB: Theater itself is already a powerful alternative, because—we're talking about theater that refuses to sell itself out. Many people think of theater like a sound stage for film; that is, many picture theater as a studio, and they're already imagining a comedy filmed for television. Lots of theater in Italy works this way and I imagine it's the same in America. You're already imagining the television or movie product. But if you think of it exclusively as theater, you work more on the symbology of it, and that way you can really carve out an alternative space. Today theater is the only place where you can experiment with a total alterity with regard to the systems of mass communication. The whole problem of theater today, speaking as an artist, has to do with perception; that's the central knot; I mean, the knot isn't about more or less scandalous or shocking content, because that can always be absorbed. The problem is perception—that is, the world perceived according to the visual systems that mass communication has imposed on us, you have to work in such a way as to send those systems into tilt. That's part of what my work on narration is all about, when I talk about shifting the eyes into the ears; the audience really enters into that state, where there's nothing given them to look at; it's pretty disturbing in the context of society today. Theater can work within all that invisibility, within all those possibilities. That's why dance, poetry—the moment has come when theater can recuperate all those minor arts, returning to the way it was before, no longer separating dance from poetry from text from lighting, but putting it all together; a language can become magnificently other if it respects the statute of alterity.

Then you can really experiment. I think of audiences who see Socìetas Raffaello Sanzio, a spectacle that really turns upside down all the parameters you've used so far to look at the world. They work in a dimension that is an absolute free zone. I think the reason audiences are growing for theater depends in part on this overdose of visibility, this overdose of reality. People who can feel this overdose crushing them seek out other pathways, they go to poetry readings, theater of narration, experimental theater, anything that doesn't go along with what they already know. In that sense there's great potential, like never before. But it's always that way in times of crisis, no? We talked yesterday about the baroque scales, today we're in a sort of baroque period; one world has come to an end and we don't know what's coming next. Nobody named it the baroque period while it was happening.[5]

Q: But they concentrated on form.

MB: They concentrated on form, and I think we're in a similar period today, waiting for a new classicism, if it's ever going to come, because the world could collapse, we could die as a species. This is something new too; humans have never faced a problem like this before. The Cold War was terrible, but it was about technology. Now it feels as though our very way of proceeding in the world has slipped from our grasp. This feeling of looming apocalypse is very interesting theatrically too, as long as it doesn't turn into a facile apocalypse, like *The Da Vinci Code*, where it just becomes an appealing visual. But if, within your work, you manage to perceive that we're in a moment when everything could come to an end, not simply one era giving way to another, but the world itself could end, it's very interesting from a linguistic point of view.

Q: This reminds me of the so-called New Italian Epic, because if you isolate certain elements of what you've been saying, such as art born of conflict, your theater born of conflict, the hypothesis of using a different language, the specter of the apocalypse, the possibility of intervening in the polis, these are the parameters of the manifesto of the New Italian Epic, which you've said you admire but that you're critical of as well.[6] I'd like to know what are the theoretical differences between your theater and this new trend, which is self-baptized, self-canonized, as Benedetti says.

MB: Well, first of all I'm glad that the word "epic" has returned to use. "Epic" had been totally removed from the dictionary for years [laughs], after the 1970s no one used the word, if you did you were an old reactionary. So now I'm glad the word has come back because it presupposes the need for a story made of stories. Because the epic is not a story, it's a story made of stories. An epic doesn't answer the question, "How did history go?" but rather, "How might it have gone if it hadn't gone as it did?" That's the epic, that possibility. . . . It's a world in which the textual, linguistic work, the work of construction, is horizontal, not vertical. This is the big difference. It's about the possibility of digression, the possibility of getting lost inside your story, like *The Odyssey, The Iliad*. It's not of the Renaissance—that is, it's not a journey toward an objective, toward a vanishing point. So from that viewpoint I'm glad they've brought the word back. But it's a problem of codes, so to speak, in that I don't care for definitions, I don't admire the effort to . . . because in Italy—maybe everywhere—as soon as you fence off an area, everybody tries to cluster into it, so you end up impeding any real encounter. I mean, they could have spoken about epic without having to define who was epic and who wasn't.

Q: And it would have been more instructive too.

MB: That's the part that doesn't work for me, because it turns into marketing, rather than something real. Anyway, there are a lot of writers they don't name who are more epic than they are.

Q: That's what Carla Benedetti says, too.

MB: Right! That's what's weird about it, the fact that you create this formula and immediately you've decided who's in and who's out; this is very Italian. It happened with the theater of narration, civil theater, image theater, the Third Theater, and it happens in literature and cinema.[7] It's a shame because the definition always hides something, but no matter what, you've still gotten close to the problem, no? Speaking of epic, it would be interesting to explore why there's a need for epic, whereas who is doing epic seems less interesting to me. Rather, what do we mean by epic?

Q: Because epic, traditionally, is also celebratory, but the epic people talk about in Italy today is not.

MB: Right, and then there's the risk that it turns into . . . I'm always feeling the presence of the postmodern, as though with the New Epic, we can permit ourselves to tell stories about anything whatsoever. "You take 1954, I'll take 1980, you take Pocahontas . . ." The important thing is to make the writing very appealing and popular; you use the techniques of pulp fiction rather than the nineteenth-century popular novel. But I ask myself, "If everything goes, then why do it at all?" I think epic should be just the opposite of that; you can't do a lot of them in a single life, you can only do one or two, and those one or two have to deal with urgent matters for you as an artist. When I meet these people, I want to ask, "Why did you recount the epic tale of Pocahontas?" It has nothing to do with me, with my country. I mean, it's a beautiful read, I can read it on the train, I read it for entertainment. But to call that a new epic seems a lot to ask, no? It would be great to create an epic that deals with your own country or with the Western world. That is, deal with the places where our dead are buried . . . but this stuff is New Age literature. Our dead are here in Italy, so you either talk about that, or what are you really doing?

Q: This reminds me of your *Black Pinocchio* project, in the sense that the New Epic is about lowering of the idea of the national intellectual, whether Italian, French, etc. Perhaps reality is more global now.[8]

MB: Yes, and that's good, so long as we understand we must investigate our Western culture in a global sense, our Western culture and the conflicts it produces . . .

Q: The opposite of what Pocahontas does, practically, whereas *Black Pinocchio* is an Italian national product that has been somehow exported . . .

MB: And gets contaminated, it gets dirty.

Q: . . . contaminated, while Pocahontas is the opposite.

MB: Pocahontas is the opposite, but this is something I have to work out better, to understand what's going on . . .

Q: You spoke about the dead, which leads me to think about the question of commemoration. Returning to *Body of State*, which was a work born with a commemorative function, and now May 9 is being proposed as a . . .

MB: Why shouldn't it be?

Q: You get summoned to perform it . . . what does this moment of commemoration represent for you? A commemoration, an act of memory; what is that for you?

MB: Commemoration is an act of co-memory, a sharing of memories. I'm reminded of when I met Ismail Kadarè, the Albanian writer who won the Nobel Prize, brilliant and quite old. I invited him to take part in the Ports of the Mediterranean project, and he came out with this observation: that theater was not born from Dionysian festivals, but from mourning rituals. Very provocative: the first form of theater were the professional mourners, the village women who were summoned to grieve and recount the life of the dead person . . .

[Maria Maglietta arrives.]

Ismail Kadarè explained that these women mourned passionately, better than the dead person's actual relatives, so they were summoned because their grief was more powerful than that of the relatives; in fact, it was a theatrical performance. They were hired to commemorate the dead, and through that commemoration, naturally, they returned the dead person to the living, enlarging his or her capacities, like in the *Odyssey* when it recounts the great dead; it's the same mechanism. It's interesting to think of theater born not from Dionysian festivals but from grief; maybe it's not true, but it sets up an interesting mechanism. That's what commemoration is for me, but you can only do it in certain moments and with certain symbols; only with certain dead. There needs to be an aura around the dead body, even if that aura was created by the mass media, evoked by everything that happened around the death. For example, the death of the child, Alfredino Rampi, that is a death with an aura around it, no question. The problem remains of how to recount it, how to handle it. These are the events that mark historical passages . . .

Q: My question is about the professional mourners, who didn't necessarily know the dead person but managed to render his or her life more real than the relatives. [To Maria Maglietta] Yesterday you talked about the piece you did in which you recounted in first person the life of a woman who had lived an epic life, and you had to invent moments in her life as a child. Then she came to see the performance, and she recognized herself in those invented moments?

MM: Exactly.

Q: This woman saw your account of her life, and you made up episodes of her life, and she recognized herself in those moments. In what way did she recognize herself?

MM: Rather than inventing episodes from thin air, I made the episodes visible; that is, if she was an adolescent who did certain things, I performed that adolescent physically, with a body, a voice, not knowing whether it was her, in the sense that it was my own dramaturgical interpretation. This section came right before a very tragic moment in the piece, when the Nazis murdered a group of civilians, and she finds herself face to face with an SS captain. So I needed a lighter moment beforehand, a moment in the piece when the audience could laugh, even. I felt very nervous that she'd say, "What are you doing? I wasn't like that at all." I mean, it's one thing to write down an episode, but something else to perform it. When you perform it there's a body, someone speaking and moving, that renders the moment more alive. But when she saw it she said, "I was just like that!" And she was a woman . . .

MB: Quite a woman!

MM: Yes, when she was young, after the war, she became Miss Italia, because she was . . .

MB: . . . beautiful.

MM: . . . a Gina Lollobrigida type. She called me "Piccolina" ["Little One"] because she was . . . well, now she's become more robust, but then, blue-green eyes, tall, very . . .

MB: . . . twice Maria's size!

MM: "I was just like that!" she said. It's beautiful! For example, after the show . . . I almost always perform it barefoot, but afterward people tell me, "You seemed so much taller on stage!" I don't know why, something must take place on stage; even she said so, even though I'm much darker than she is. But I had to perform what she imagined, making it visible, including even a time before she was born.

MB: This word time [in Italian, "time"—*tempo*—can signify also musical tempo—ed.] is extremely interesting. Maria didn't invent episodes from thin air rather, she simply introduced time into what was written on the page. That's what happens in theater. You read something written, it says, "She went from here to there, she did this and that," but when you perform it on stage, what's written takes on biological time that doesn't correspond at all to the time it took to read that line of text; you read it in a second, but it takes some time to perform.

MM: It's a reinvention!

MB: So what do you fill that time with? Performing those lines, the body of the actress makes them into something that is a total invention with respect to the writing. The content is the same, but in the theater that content suddenly slips, no? It fills with living time, the time of the actress. And that actress planned that she needed a moment of lightness before the catastrophe, although that lightness wasn't in the book, but she made the artistic choice to create a moment when the public could smile.

MM: For example, the author only dedicates a few lines to her mother, who spent nearly her entire life in a sanatorium, but every so often I evoke the mother by acting her out, even adding a piece of Bohemian music, so with just a few gestures I sketch out the story of her mother, who had been . . .

MB: . . . tuberculosis.

MM: . . . abandoned by this man, she was a skilled laborer, but unable to work because of her disease, who raised this little girl on her own, and was very badly thought of by everyone because she'd had a baby with a man considered irresponsible, and who had then disappeared. It was a delicate situation and I was very nervous about it, because she could have objected . . . that is, her own mother was a myth to her, because she had lived far away from her; they had very few moments of reconciliation. But there too, she felt that I was really telling her true story; it was incredible. I was much more emotionally moved than when I deal with other kinds of works, because this woman was present, alive, so I was very concerned not to offend her sensibilities.

MB: It was like the night when Giorgio's mother came to see *Body of State*.

Q: I've been wanting to ask you about the tempo of *Body of State*, both the time and the tempo. It stands out in *Body of State* because it's a condensation of a written text, or rather, the written text is something else, a variation on the oral text, but in performance in various moments you begin by saying, "But this isn't the story I want to tell you this evening." This is what Calvino does in *The Path to the Spider's Nest*, which became a manifesto for neorealism.[9] He has many beginnings: he begins, tells a story, goes off in one direction; this too is a matter of orality because he speaks of orality too. He talks about all the stories people told during the Resistance, but then he says, "But this isn't what I want to talk about, I want to talk about something else." I'd like to know what is the function of this continuous beginning over again. Is it simply a technical device, or is it your intention to carry the audience in a certain direction in order to say certain things? What things, and what directions?

MB: It's like what we were saying earlier about the function of epic. An epic continuously makes present all the possibilities in a story; this is what the great epic structures do. There is not cause and effect consequentiality between what comes before and what comes after. There's a before, it begins, but that "before" has many "befores" before it. That is, a "before" takes off in one direction, but then suddenly you lose it; a different story begins, but then you return and take it up again, but then there's yet another beginning. Or you might always allude to the possibility that "I'm only telling you this part, but there's also another part I could tell you." For example, in *Body of State* when I say, "You could tell this like a story between fathers and sons"; that could be a whole other story. It's the art of digression, which is wrapped up with the epic.

Q: Because neorealism is a selection of these possibilities.

MB: In the traditional novel, you have a character who develops, A, B, C, to the end, no? In epic, instead, this character departs, but then he begins to get lost.

Q: Horizontal and multiple.

MB: Multiple! Think of Stefano D'Arrigo's *Cino Sorta*. The main character, Cino Sorta, is a soldier at the end of the war. It takes him three days to cross the Strait of Messina. Six hundred pages for three days.

MM: No, twelve hundred pages.

MB: Twelve hundred, amazing.

MM: D'Arrigo can dedicate one hundred pages to a single instant.

MB: But it's a single instant that you experience as though that were the whole story. Like when he finds the boat on the road, no? That's what epic is. You have the opportunity to . . .

Q: The description of the shield . . .

MB: Exactly, *Seven Against Thebes*, the description of each warrior's shield, and you ask yourself, "Why this? Who needs it, I want the war!" But no, that's it, right there. The problem is getting your spectators to accept it. The real force that epic could have today is still a perceptual problem, because audiences today are totally unaccustomed to this way of unfolding a story. Audiences want it to go boom boom boom, they want communication with immediate results, they want product. Information is product, so you have to give immediate results, so in the editing, in the form, it's all tum tum tum. So when they find themselves facing someone who starts to go off in different directions, they get confused, they panic. So getting them to accept, and ultimately being able to move them and have them enjoy this sort of unfolding, is a political objective, in my opinion, because it means you've shifted them away from the perceptual conventions that society forces them to accept.

MM: I think in this particular moment this is precisely the function of art, because everything else can be done better by computers. That is, if you want some information, you can get that data almost immediately, so instead you have to refuel the imaginative possibility of saying, "This is just one part of the story, but think how many more there are." And to give birth to the desire for a world that can be infinite somehow.

Q: As a matter of fact, what I'd like to ask you now is, in what way is your theater political? Especially *Body of State*; is *Body of State* a protest, and the larger question, are you doing political theater?

MB: What do you mean by protest and what do you mean by political? For the way I think of protest, *Body of State* is not a protest. What would it be protesting? It's a spectacle that shows, that stages . . . It would have been a protest if I had made a play about conspiracy theories behind the Moro killing, such as who killed him, why, what was the role of the secret services? That is, if I'd worked investigatively, which might, in fact, have been interesting, but that wasn't the path I chose to take. That would have been a protest, and it would have been political theater. . . . In my opinion, it's already political when you use a particular kind of language, for me it's political when the spectator enters the theater and is forced to look with different eyes. When Brecht talked about alienation and Brook spoke about reawakening, Brecht was speaking in terms of content, and Brook was speaking in terms of New Age spirituality, but underneath both there is the problem of perception—that is, both needed moments within their plays when the spectators would break out of the canonical way they'd been seeing the world. This is the political function of theater. Perhaps not for the entire play, but that's what we aim for, that's the dimension our plays work on . . .

MM: It's the communicative mechanism that's political, to . . .

MB: Exactly, it's more the language I work with than . . . for example, *La Pelle* [*The Skin*] is a totally political piece, because the spectators leave the theater upset, not only because of the content of Malaparte's text, but because of the way he staged the scenes he described, how he constructed the events.

MM: It's like when Pasolini accused the *Palazzo* [Palace of Power] for the disappearance of the fireflies; political in that sense.[10]

MB: Exactly.

Q: But what was he protesting?

MB: He was using a grand metaphor. It was beautiful that he was using the fireflies as a metaphor. He didn't stand there saying, "We accuse them because they did this or that." Instead he took fireflies as a metaphor; that's art. So if that's what you mean by protest, then fine, yes. But usually in Italy, protest theater is theater that explains; that's the problem. The political theater of the '70s, and lots of theater today called civil theater, does this; it's theater that explains, protests by pointing fingers at the bad guys, or those who are responsible for certain things. I'm not saying it's useless; it can be very useful, but for me, art should go a step further.

Notes

1. Vittorio Gassman (1922–2000), stage and screen actor, was one of Italy's leading male actors for classical theater, including leading roles in Shakespeare, Tennessee Williams, and classical Greek theater.
2. For information about Baliani's works, please see the introduction.

3. On the *carabinieri*'s killing of student activist Francesco Lorusso in Bologna in March 1977, please see the introduction.

4. Baliani is referring to an article that Pier Paolo Pasolini originally wrote for the newspaper *Il Corriere della Sera* on December 9, 1973, titled "Sfida ai dirigenti della televisione" [Challenge to the Television Executives]. In 1975, Pasolini published a reduced form of this piece with the title "Acculturazione e acculturazione" [Acculturation and Acculturation] in the collection of critical essays *Scritti corsari* [*Corsair Writings*]. The full-length article, "Contro la televisione," is now included in *Tutte le opere: Saggi sulla politica e sulla società*, edited by Walter Siti and Silvia De Laude (Milan: Mondadori, 1999), 128–43.

5. The Societas Raffaello Sanzio is an avante-garde theater collective, based in Cesena, Italy and founded in 1981 by siblings Romeo and Claudia Castellucci and Romeo's spouse, Chiara Guidi. The company achieved international acclaim with its *Tragedia Endogonidia* project (2002–2004). This peripatetic performance, held in various world capitals, transformed from one venue to another.

6. New Italian Epic is a literary trend identified in 2008 by Wu Ming, a collective of authors (based in Bologna) who publish anonymously as a collective, have written *Q*, *'54*, and, most recently, *Manituana*, in which one of the characters is Pocahontas. Wu Ming attempted a rigorous definition of the features of New Italian Epic in a series of conferences held in Canada and in the United States in 2008. The pamphlet *New Italian Epic* (Turin: Einaudi, 2009) raised a heated controversy. Carla Benedetti, a literary critic and university professor, harshly contested the whole operation, accusing Wu Ming of commercial self-promotion. See "Free Italian Epic," http://www.ilprimoamore.com/testo_1376.html, accessed on May 23, 2011. A reduced version of this review was then published in *L'Espresso*, March 10–11, 2009, 118, with the title "Stroncatura epica."

7. Third Theater is a term popularized by Eugenio Barba, founder of Odin Teatret, to describe an alternative theater movement widespread in Europe in the 1970s. The form is called "Third" with respect, first, to traditional commercial theater and, second, to state-financed "serious" theater, such as the Berliner Ensemble. Third Theater companies tended to be collectives of young actors without formal stage training, who composed original pieces that violated or ignored standard theatrical conventions and technologies.

8. See the introduction for a description of Baliani's work with Nairobi homeless children, *Black Pinocchio*.

9. Italo Calvino's first work of fiction, *Il sentiero dei nidi di ragno* [*Path to the Spiders' Nest*], was published in 1947 and is considered a classic example of Italian neorealism. Please see also the introduction for Calvino's thoughts about micro-history, its role in the immediate postwar period, and the way it tallies with Baliani's vision of theater and art.

10. Baliani is referring to one of Pasolini's most famous articles, titled "Il vuoto del potere in Italia," but more popularly known as "L'articolo delle lucciole" [The Article of the Fireflies], which he wrote against the Christian Democrats on February 1, 1975, for *Il Corriere della Sera*. See "1 Febbraio 1975: L'articolo delle lucciole," in *Tutte le opere: Saggi sulla politica e sulla società*, edited by Walter Siti and Silvia De Laude (Milan: Mondadori, 1999), 404–11. Please see the introduction, where Pasolini's thoughts about the *Palazzo* as the place of hegemony are explored.

Performance, *Corpo di Stato*, Northwestern University, April 2009
(Image courtesy of the Multimedia Learning Center
of Weinberg College, Northwestern University)

Performance, *Corpo di Stato*, Northwestern University, April 2009
(Image courtesy of the Multimedia Learning Center
of Weinberg College, Northwestern University)

Performance, *Corpo di Stato*, Northwestern University, April 2009
(Image courtesy of the Multimedia Learning Center
of Weinberg College, Northwestern University)

Performance, *Corpo di Stato*, Northwestern University, April 2009
(Image courtesy of the Multimedia Learning Center
of Weinberg College, Northwestern University)

Afterword

Marco Baliani and Maria Maglietta

Encounters

The encounter between students and lecturers during each of our academic experiences was different according to each of our host colleges' "style," but always intense. By "style" we refer to the particular way in which each single college is related to its environment, the different languages it speaks, the representational codes it lives by and its history.

The theatrical performance *Body of State* always led students to take two positions: on one side, there are those who are more interested in the historical content of the story because of their knowledge of the matter and their interest in knowing more about what happened in those years in Italy.

Their interest impressed us. Some of them were well aware of what we were talking about because of the way they study in those colleges. It is as if they were constantly expanding on certain topics, dissecting them for their own knowledge.

Some other students, the majority, were moved by the way the performance was presented and by the fact that an adult, a pretty old one, was there, putting out there the person he was many years before.

Just like a child loves listening to adults telling stories about their childhood, students were amazed by an adult talking about his life as a student in a different time and in a different world.

These two ways of interacting with the performance were the main ones and were similar in every situation, though different in the ways they were shown, perceived and related.

Someone rarely tried to investigate on the pattern of the performance, or better, the dramaturgical/theatrical mode it had been built on. Even when dealing with acting students, the interest in this sort of concern was minor. The same thing happens in Italy too. *Body of State* is a performance strongly defined by its historical content, by the memory of a recent past and the intense content of the memories it exposes. This last aspect overshadows the perception of more technical aspects, which is something that doesn't happen in other performances, such as *Kohlhaas*, where the actor's corporeal narration requires an interface with the language and the theatrical/dramaturgical construction.

Body of State's unfolding, and its even slower and more concise rhythm due to subtitles, mitigated the divide, emphasizing the content more than in the Italian version of the performance, where the rhythm of some passages, such as the demonstration, produces strong emotional empathy. This is particularly interesting, since it shows, once again, how theater is a true, absolute, live performance that changes and modifies according to the physical, concrete conditions of the audience, the space and the relations that are built between these elements.

The animated sequence of encounters we had, the busy days during which we were always engaged doing something, makes it hard to remember every single place we visited. We have the feeling that we had close encounters of the third or fourth kind, that we actually met aliens. These students, so focused on being students, will be the leading class of a huge country, whose size we were able to measure by the differences between places, distant from each other both in space and substance. We were able to get close to a generation for which communication is difficult. This is exactly what characterizes the colleges we visited while touring the United States. They enclose a generation, so to speak, religiously; they "re-ligunt"—that is, circumscribe, foster, and preserve it until their inevitable separation—and they do so knowing they are responsible for shaping their young students' lives.

This transcends the mere subjects taught and areas of study. It is as if there were a preceding condition that forces students and lecturers to some kind of unspoken agreement, an invisible though very strong tie.

Style

In New York, the city camouflages the university, just like Italy, where universities have a symbiotic relationship with their home cities. In the United States, this symbiotic relationship is beneficial mostly to the big city whose chaos swallows everything. There are so many things to do and so many visual, audio and tactile stimuli, that it is hard not to be dragged into the city's whirl. Students here seem to be just tourists, strangers trying to focus on their studies, creating free zones, tribes, places where they can actually recognize each other and establish bonds of friendship.

The other universities we visited are cities unto themselves. They are autonomous, self-sufficient, and self-referential and this really impressed us. On the other side of the fence, the "real" towns are much less "real," solid and authentic. They seem to stretch out of shape and, with no real connection to the college world, get lost. They seem palpably inferior to that world in such a way that makes the population appear as part of a different America. In fact, despite their differences from one another, universities are the prerogative of an elite that is sometimes stronger and wealthier than the community that surrounds it. This caused a constant feeling of disorientation, as if we were in a world where everything works perfectly and is within reach, from the fancy fitness center to the football field and the library, to the theaters and labs, and so on. Each place has been efficiently built in order to be used to the best of its capabilities. Spaces are didactic instruments per se and force the students to feel the need to be there. There are no exits and no distractions save those the students make for themselves, coherently within the system of the college that houses and binds them.

In Bloomington, at Indiana University, the first college we visited, the size of the buildings was overwhelming. We felt that our enthusiastic welcome was due to the fact that travelers' visits are similar to the relationships between *clerici vagantes* and monks. A historically recurring exchange that allows the students to feel as though they are on their own, an island in the middle of a flat plain that could be more or less extended. An island or a huge monastery where there's a tangible curiosity for everything that is outside.

The presence of a social "caste" is missing here. People come and go and everyone is busy taking care of things outside of the academic sphere. But this may not be true; it could be that the megalopolis-like way of life at the college produces such a mix of people and activities that you feel as though you were in a real city. We feel that our presence there was valuable, as we feel it was everywhere we went, and our contribution was soon absorbed through an effective, well-tested procedure.

The "style" of the second college we visited—Wesleyan, Middletown, Connecticut—was totally different. Here, again, we had the feeling of being on an island. More than in our previous experience, the surrounding town was made up of a series of streets like those you see in road movies, without a real "old town," a "center," as in Carson McCullers's *The Ballad of the Sad Café*. Though we were not in the South, it felt like we were. If tumbleweeds had blown by the wind, it would have seemed like another part of America. At the borders of this unreal city is the strong, resolute and "true" city, more austere and, as we would say, more religious. Here there was a clearer sense of belonging to a special class, with a certain rigor and method. Even the meetings and gatherings were planned as tools of learning. We felt that our arrival had been prepared for and anticipated for some time and consequently our reception was immediate and fruitful. We met with a group of acting students and, when we talked about the tradition of storytelling, we saw their surprise and disorientation. In fact, they had many questions for us afterward.

For the third visit at Dickinson College (Carlisle, Pennsylvania), the style was more our own in the sense of a sort of vital confusion, an overlapping of meetings—some flowing from others that had not been planned—with great enthusiasm and human warmth. It was here more than in other places that we were asked about our past: who we were, where we came from, if we had children, and so on. It was as if there was a dimension of the university that was more familial, a social cohesion stemming not only from study but also from the layout of the campus, student housing, coffeehouses. Outside the invisible fence we did not perceive the presence of another town except perhaps as places in service to the university.

We have spoken of an invisible fence because in reality the universities have no limits or barriers, except for Yale, to which we turn below. It was as if the boundary of the university was indicated by motion sensors like those you would find around the perimeter of the garden of a private house. This could be an American feature *tout court*: the gardens don't have picket fences but the picket fence is there just the same and is as rigid—if not more so—as a real fence. Could this sense of boundaries and property have been passed down by the pioneers?

In Vermont, at Middlebury College, we had still other sensations. Beyond the college is this little town living in an ecological dimension that seems out of step with the times, bordered by stupendous landscapes. It's the lifestyle of ex–flower children now living institutionalized lives but still in a sort of 1970s atmosphere, down to the stores and the way people greet and speak to you. At the same time, there's the sense of an illusion of living in a frontier post, just a few steps away from the wildlife that really does not exist anymore but still lives in the imagination. The college breathes this freespiritedness but, at the same time, seems more solid and structured than the world around it. It feels it must show that it hasn't allowed itself to be seduced by that dreamy pace and is instead determined, active, productive. Here more than elsewhere we got the sense that the college was composed of bodies, of physicality, of athletic practices and rehearsals and races and swimming pools. It was as if it responded to the outside world in all its solid and physical corporeality.

We were welcomed quickly, intensely and deeply, with great warmth.

At Northwestern, the university campus is in Evanston, quite separate and distant from the center of Chicago. Chicago's city center is vital and substantial. We couldn't meet with groups of students and the performance, like at

Wesleyan and at the Casa Italiana Zerilli-Marimò at New York University, was open to the public, albeit in nontraditional spaces. In each of these places the discussion afterward took on a more political character, owing also to the many Italians who were present, as if the performance offered an excuse to talk about now and not so much the 1970s.

We had no meetings at Yale that weren't related to our gig and for this reason we can't say much save for the stupefying impression of having been at the center of a totalizing stage set. The omnipresent architecture that had molded everything in its own style—even the rest of the city that seems, in contrast, like some sort of a guest house, only more opaque and imitative. The fortress that teems with Gothic spires and niches and hyper-technological libraries seems to gather in itself the very mystery of study and knowledge. The atmosphere here is truly monastic, meant for secret sects and initiates, but this is only the first impression. In reality, here, as elsewhere, this showy architecture serves to concentrate the mind on the course of study that has been chosen.

Varied Sensations

In the end what we decided was that America is too big to be able to understand. There are too many Americas. In the face of such diversity, for those who, like us, come from a country you can measure and traverse entirely in a few days, the feeling is one of disorientation and dismay.

In New York, in Chicago, and in a lesser way Washington, we asked ourselves if it would ever be possible for Americans to learn to consume less than they throw away on a daily basis. We think probably not. Cities are a constant incentive for bulimia, more visual than alimentary. The excess of food and sweets and drinks is nothing more than the result of a bulimia of the senses that passes first through the eye, which is constantly exhorted to desire, devour, take, visit, query, grasp.

It is hard to imagine that world without the waste of energy of those immense screens that take up the sides of entire skyscrapers. What sort of political education could ever teach this multitude of young people to reduce their own voracity? And what sort of future economy could prevent the current rush to the production of energy? And yet we all know and feel that continuing this way is impossible, but nothing crops up to bravely sign a different way. On the other hand, the hordes of tourists that swarm the centers of these megalopolises seek the very thrills that the cities offer, like some sort of perennial amusement park.

Joking around one day we said to each other that Americans are morphing into a populace that can live with just one arm or hand: the other one is permanently occupied by a huge cup of some hyper-caloric drink filled with sugar and rigorously frozen.

You always work while you eat, while you talk and converse. You eat constantly: continuous breaks, snacks, cookies. The moment of food is a rapid passage of words, without really ever really tasting what you're swallowing, as if you didn't have enough time. It could be that this quick tempo permeates one's entire existence, imminent, pressing. It has already been incorporated and has become an existential modality of life.

Theater

Always acting, interpreting, identifying with, Actors' Studio. It seemed this way to us, based on what we saw, both in terms of schools and professional performances. There are, we are sure, other points of view, but the presence of an interpretive structure of the Actor's Studio is clearly felt. This means that theater remains above all a result of writing, of an author, of plot and narrative. It is as if, facing the multi-form reality of the world that the cities and universities offer and in which they are immersed, they needed a representational structure that was very traditional and solid, and as if the theater was a place in which one could still circumscribe the world in the pretense of an ancient and contradictory spatial-temporal unity with respect to the glowing game of the external perceptions. It's something to think about.

Marco Baliani and Maria Maglietta
New York, May 10, 2009

Appendix: Reviews
A FULL SET OF NEW STORIES: THE RECEPTION OF MARCO BALIANI AND MARIA MAGLIETTA'S NORTH AMERICAN TOUR, SPRING 2009

Marco Baliani and Maria Maglietta toured the United States in the spring of 2009 with performances of different properties at several different universities. Collected here are reviews of *Body of State* from the different venues. The itinerary included the following stops in the following order: Indiana University; Wesleyan University; Dickinson College; the Italian Cultural Institute of Washington, D.C.; Yale University; Middlebury College; Northwestern University, the Italian Cultural Institute of Chicago; and New York University.

The reviewers come from all corners of the university: undergraduates, graduate students, professors of all ranks from departments of literature, theater, government, art history, some Italian, some American, some from other cultures and cultural stories. They wrote about their experience as spectators of *Body of State* or about their participation in the workshops and lectures that Marco and Maria held during the tour. A mixed bag or a melting pot? Probably a bit of each. These reviews of the different performances of *Body of State* give birth to a full set of new "stories."

The order of these reviews follows the chronology of the tour, beginning with Indiana University on April 12, 2009 (Easter Sunday), and concluding in New York City with a performance at New York University, in conjunction with the American Association of Italian Studies on May 8, 2009. All performances featured projected supertitles in English, the translation of *Body of State* included here. Maria Maglietta was both technical director and director and ran the computer, lights, and soundboard at performances, assisted by the local staff.

The spaces for performance—and the pieces for performance—differed from one place to the next. The reviews collected here concern *Body of State*, though Baliani presented on *Pinocchio Nero* (Dickinson College, the Italian

Cultural Institute of Chicago, and Middlebury College) and also discussed his film performances (Yale) during the tour. At Indiana University, the performance space was a traditional—and enormous—auditorium with moveable seats and theatrical lighting. At Dickinson, the performance took place at the "Cube," a solo-actor theater, with theatrical lights, a two-screen system for subtitles, and an intimate, dark atmosphere that was ideal for *Body of State*, Baliani said. At Wesleyan, *Body of State* was open to the public and performed in a steep cinema, which was excellent for the projection of the supertitles in English as well as the video montage, but where the lighting was not theatrical. These conditions, Baliani says, are common for the performance of this piece. At Northwestern, Baliani performed in a small auditorium with a thrust stage and theatrical lighting, and, at New York University's Casa Italiana Zerilli-Marimò, the concluding performance, in a small auditorium.

If the spaces for performance differed, so did the audiences, both in size as well as in constitution. At NYU, for example, the event was open to the public but, in contrast to the audiences elsewhere during the tour, was largely seen by Italianists from universities throughout the United States (and abroad) who were attending the annual conference of the American Association of Italian Studies. The conference featured a roundtable discussion the day following Baliani's performance: "Resistere narrando," or resist by narrating. The roundtable was dedicated to the theater of narration—especially Baliani's—and the culture of the *denuncia*, or, the "J'accuse!" characteristic of Emile Zola's denunciation of the French government's persecution of Alfred Dreyfus in a letter published in the French newspaper *L'Aurore* in 1898 in what is usually referred to as the Dreyfus Affair. The Sicilian writer and MP Leonardo Sciascia famously reprised Zola's accusation in his minority report on the investigation of the Moro kidnapping and assassination, calling it *L'Affaire Moro*.

Reception of *Body of State* depended on a variety of factors, including the material conditions of performance, like the kind of space used and lighting, but also on a set of expectations that included preparation (both educational and cultural), age, linguistic competence, and ideology.

These reviews constitute a unique, and often difficult to attain, archival documentation of Baliani's tour with *Body of State*. Patricia Di Silvio (Tufts University) notes in her comments that "this collection of written responses to the performance in the present volume constitutes an extension [of the theatricalization of memorialization of the struggles], producing a kind of multi-faceted hypertext for re-evoking the experience of Baliani's one-man show." The comments' presentation here accumulates in rhythm and energy, very much like the tour itself, culminating in New York. We did not censor these comments, though we did ensure stylistic coherence between and among them.

Journaling the Experience: Indiana University, Performance and Residency. Bloomington (April 9–13, 2009)

The preparations were many, they started a year earlier. The flurry of excitement in the three to four weeks before their visit was great and rapidly reaching a crescendo as some 400 undergraduates taking Italian planned to attend what was for many their first live monologue theater performance.

I. THE VISIT

Curtain

The Arrival

Marco Baliani and Maria Maglietta arrive in Bloomington, Indiana, on Easter Sunday, 2009. They are visibly excited and immediately engaged. They are curious about campus life and ready for action. It is relatively late on Sunday, the theater is closed, so we can't yet address our first priority, that of getting to "know" the theater space. So we get to know each other instead. We talk in detail about their two-day itinerary, the technical set-up, the performance, the post-performance talk. We also consider the audience and nature of the two teaching events that Marco and Maria will lead—one a lesson in the Italian Theater Workshop course, the other a two-hour, open-door roundtable for graduate students of Italian and other fields. Our guests begin to gain a sense of place, objectives, and rhythm. A bit later, after a meal, they're off to sleep.

Day 1

10 a.m. The Theater Space

Marco and Maria get into the theater space. It is a very large, wood-lined auditorium, with high ceilings and old, wooden stage. Marco walks around, Marco explores, Marco asks for Maria's input every step of the way. Will he play on stage or on the floor? On the stage? Will the spotlight be sufficient, can it move to follow him all right? Will we use one screen or two for the subtitles and images? Two. Can we find a stool or a chair? Yes. No, that's not the right one—too bourgeois, too modern. There, the older, simpler wooden one in the student café next door. Can we borrow it? Sure. The mise-en-scène is quite simple. Marco recites a bit, continuing to gauge distance from audience, voice projection without microphone initially, and depth of the stage. Maria provides feedback and gathers a comprehensive sense of the auditorium as gathering space. We decide on an arrangement for the 400 chairs. We decide for semi-circle rows starting just 10 feet back from the stage. We try to render the large space more intimate. Eventually some 40 students will sit on the floor too, just under the stage.

Marco and Maria settle in for the day. No lunch break. Just work, preparations, and short breaks. Questions, answers, short experiments, deliberations, decisions.

1 p.m. The Technicians

A great team of union technicians arrives to help with lights and microphone, projectors, computers and screens. It takes about two hours to get everything set. Spot size, spot movements, projector lights versus spot lights, sound projection from the stage, computer image size visibility, computer table position, and timing of slide change. Marco and Maria are communicating in English. The technicians, a jolly, open-minded bunch, are doing their best to understand and fill-in-blanks in the conversation. They never lose patience or cool, even if we are moved by an inch 12 or 15 times in a row. We have had a successful intercultural experience. Things are coming together nicely. Marco seems a bit nervous but also pleased. Maria too.

4 p.m. All Is Set

It's time to leave them alone. Marco and Maria need space. There are two hours until the show. Rehearse, relax, review, unwind. A coffee, a distraction, another rehearsal. Full concentration mode now. No intrusions or interruptions until the doors open at 5:50 for a performance at 6.

5:50 p.m. A Hundred or So Students Are Already at the Door

They come in, they sit toward the back, we invite them closer. They read the program. At 6 p.m. the 300 regular seats are filled. Staff arrive to bring 50 more seats. Other students line up on the sides of the theater. Others still, invited by Marco himself, already on stage, come to sit up front on the floor.

6:05–7:30 p.m. Body of State

The performance was excellent. It came off without a hitch. The audience was riveted. The scene about the hand bombs and Marco's confusion was their favorite.

7:30–8:15 p.m. Post-performance Conversation and Reception

About 50 people remained to meet Marco and Maria and to ask a few questions or discuss the performance with others. This began more formally with everyone sitting in the first rows of the auditorium. Marco and Maria were eager to engage. After about 10 minutes here, the group was invited to the reception room where broader, less formal conversation took place and students could, one by one, meet and speak informally with our guests.

First Impressions: The entire day was exhilarating from start to finish. I learned so much about Marco's pre-performance preparation work and the different phases of intense concentration mitigated by occasional moments of relaxation or simple reflection. The audience was greater than what we had expected and the students, even those with very little Italian language, were riveted for the whole length of the production.

Day 2

Marco and Maria's main appointments on the second day of their visit were two. The first an open-forum discussion with graduate students on the subject of "Italian Theater Today." Since most attendees (on and off 10–12 people, since they came on rotating schedules) were Italian, we conducted the conversation in Italian. In the course of this conversation, Marco and Maria answered questions and offered varied and detailed insights on the genres that have more or less success in Italy at this time, the development of the monologue as sub-genre, the economic status of "teatri stabili," or municipally funded and permanent theaters, and independently run operations. A lunch with graduate students working on 20th-century literature and film topics followed.

Marco and Maria's second commitment was to teach the 400-level Italian Theater Workshop class. In this course, some 17 undergraduates ranging from their sophomore to senior years, were working in both on and off-stage roles to produce Fo's *La Marcolfa* as well as scenes from Goldoni's *La Locandiera* and scenes from De Filippo's *Sabato, domenica e lunedì*. Marco and Maria divided the class time (90 minutes) in half. In the first half they invited the students (approximately ten days away from their performance date) to perform scenes from their various works. Much to my surprise, none of the students was inhibited and all did their very best work for our guests. Marco and Maria enjoyed themselves thoroughly, watching with expressions of great marvel as these students, some of whom had had only three semesters of Italian, worked with dialect and regional pronunciation—these students, none of whom was an "actor" by nature or a theater-oriented person! Next, in a very inspiring fashion, Marco and Maria, each in their turn, chose small moments in each scene on which to focus for various nuances in movement, facial expression, subtle handling of objects in the scene. The students were responsive and their great and wholly positive set of emotions was virtually palpable.

During the second half of the lesson Marco and Maria worked together to present and then model the notion of theatrical rhythm and timing. Drawing upon examples from the performance of *Body of State* from the night before, Marco experimented with the students and their interpretative abilities by re-proposing the same snippet of his work with different combinations of rhythm. The students were active and accurate in grasping the concepts. Finally, Marco asked the students to apply some of the notions and variations on timing to short parts of the scenes from Fo, Goldoni, and De Filippo he had observed earlier. The class got a standing ovation. Without exaggeration, it was clear they had created a profound and absolutely memorable learning experience for all involved.

After Marco and Maria take leave ever so affectionately from the students and wish many *merdas*, or "break a leg," for their show, they are whisked away by their airport limousine. Destination? Wesleyan University.

Curtain

II. FIRST IMPRESSIONS . . . LASTING IMPRESSIONS

Marco Baliani—the man, the author, his text—had a major impact on the Indiana University community. It is not only rare that so much of our faculty and student body come together for a cultural event, but it is also rare that we ask so many to encounter "up close" a tragic moment in history such as Italian terrorism, or the years of lead. The average undergraduate may have a general sense of 20th-century European history and the Italian major a somewhat greater sense of chronology, thanks to the study of literature, film, and other texts, but relatively few have had the opportunity to read about and digest the depth and significance of political violence in Italy, nor consider how such events relate to the very recent concept of terrorism in international relations today.

One undergraduate senior, Stephen Hiller, encapsulated his personal encounter with this new cultural reality for him this way:

> I thought *Body of State* was excellent. Marco Baliani recounted such
> a volatile time in Italy's social and political history and made me
> feel as though I was living it with him. Through his performance,
> I could see and understand the pain and confusion of the Italian
> public at the time. At the end, I had gained a huge insight into
> Italy's modern history.

On the subject of the performance—its content and impact—one of our graduate student instructors remarked that

> Marco Baliani's visit to IU was both culturally enlightening and artis-
> tically educational. Mr. Baliani's monologue *Body of State*, a histori-
> cal account of the Aldo Moro tragedy, made an evident impact on its

audience through his self-interrogation and story-telling technique. While his show included English subtitles, his incorporation of images, sound, vocal intonation and expressive movements rendered the translation unnecessary, as he communicated his message clearly and with frightening truth.

The conviction that Marco's performance was both penetrating and forceful was felt all around. For the students in one Intensive Beginning Italian class, the show catalyzed both cross-cultural comparisons and personal reflections. Ermanno Conti, in his role as instructor, stated,

> Marco Baliani's visit was a privilege. It allowed my students to attend a live theatre performance in Italian—by one of the most important Italian actors of our time. They learned about a fundamental period in Italy's recent history. I had enthusiastic feedback from my students after attending the performance. One young woman from Sri Lanka said that she could identify with Marco's emotions because her country is often fraught with terrorist acts and the ongoing threat. On another note, a theater major said that Marco's performance helped confirm her wish to specialize in the monologue genre.
>
> Such testimonies give credence to the power of art in general to reach a broad audience and provide an in-person, up-close experience with another culture. If our inter-cultural goals include guiding students toward an ability to see the target culture through the lens of a native, or insider, to briefly wear his or her shoes, so to speak, then Marco's performance was extremely effective in achieving it.

There was equally enthusiastic consensus about the importance of Marco and Maria's visit from our graduate student population, particularly those working in the field of modern Italian literature and film. Doctoral candidate Emanuela Pecchioli was able to make important connections between contemporary Italian theater and certain theoretical texts she was reading for her dissertation:

> The meetings with Marco Baliani and Maria Maglietta last April, before and after the performance of *Body of State* and, of course, the performance itself were interesting for me, because they added to what has become for me a series of unplanned but very important and significant encounters with "theater" during my PhD experience. Last year, for instance, I worked on Rousseau's and Diderot's reflections on theater. It was stimulating not only to see how Diderot's *Paradoxe sur le comédien* is still valid and valuable in contemporary theater but also, and especially, to be able to ask questions about this

text to author/actor. The whole of this "theater" experience has been significant for me and I shall continue to work on theater, cinema, and acting in my research.

Similarly, doctoral candidate Ermanno Conti commented on the relationship between Baliani's performance and his research, since his dissertation treats the subject of political violence in Italian literature. In Conti's words,

> I was very fortunate to meet in person one of the authors that I am going to consider in my PhD dissertation. I am working on how literature has described and interpreted the years of lead, and Baliani's *Body of State* is one of the works I am analyzing. Thanks to Professor Ryan, I also had the opportunity to have a private meeting with Baliani. We discussed his work, his personal experience during the 1970s, and other works of literature he considers important on the subject. He also offered his availability in case I need help and/or materials for my work. Finally, his informal talk with the faculty and graduate students on Day 2 of his visit, was very important since it provided an overview of contemporary Italian theatre from the point of view one of its protagonists.

The first-hand insights gained by students working on subjects related to modern literature, theater or political science were both helpful and varied. But I would venture to say that the deepest and most lasting impressions left by Marco and Maria on the Bloomington campus were those in the minds and hearts of the undergraduates in the Italian Theater Workshop course. From one day to the next they found themselves face-to-face with and performing for professional actors and directors from their esteemed target culture: Italy. As then sophomore (with only three semesters of previous Italian language) Annie Walters recounts,

> Upon entering class, my fellow cast members and I gave a rushed and nervous performance of the first scene from Fo's *La Marcolfa*. The nervousness was due to the amount of celebrity in the room. After nerves had subsided, Baliani gave excellent commentary. He advised us to perform the play differently each time. He didn't mean with major differences like blocking but in reference to our intention and delivery. He also pointed out a sad truth, which was that we had all become used to giving the same, calculated reactions to each new event. Though I was still awe-struck at this point, Baliani's advice really helped. After our class, and in the week remaining until our performance, I felt there was a lot more room for me to explore options with the character Marcolfa. Through his help I found a more genuine and, thus, better character and style to give to the audience.

Agreeing with Annie, another actor, Stephen Hiller (of senior standing and also cast in a leading role), states,

> It was a pleasure to have such a prominent figure in Italian theater working with us trying to help us improve our skills such as they were. And rather than giving particular notes, he provided more general advice that could help us with not only the scenes we showed him but with our movements and performances as a whole. The combination of seeing Marco perform and then provide suggestions for techniques and other comments that he had brought to life in his own performance the night before, really helped me think about my performance and how to improve it.

The courage but also the spontaneity of the undergraduate theater group was quickly apparent to all. I attribute their lack of inhibition (despite underlying nervousness) to Marco and Maria's assuring tone, friendly faces and genuine curiosity about what we do and how at the American university. It was as if the students felt they could share a bit of their own persons back. Mary Migliorelli was the graduate student assistant director for the workshop course and production. From her perspective she adds that

> I was also fortunate enough to witness Marco Baliani and Maria Maglietta in a classroom setting where they generously shared their theatrical expertise with my Italian theatre students. Their suggestions on comical timing, tone and movement served as a great aide to the actors and our production and displayed the variety of talent these two professionals possess. We were all so grateful for Baliani and Maglietta's visit; it was a truly unforgettable experience.

"An unforgettable experience." I think this says it all, particularly for the smaller theater workshop group. Even if comprised entirely of amateur players and non-theater department students, the members of the course were, by this time in the semester, wholly dedicated to their collaborative project and the quality and impact of their own public performance. The absolutely friendly and encouraging faces of Marco and Maria quickly dissolved the affective barrier and what took place was a workshop exercise. Our "maestri," or teachers, revisited stage movements, interactions with props, and facial expressions, all under the rubric of rhythm and timing. Whereas students had, up to now, focused on memorizing lines, interpreting characters and remembering the bigger basics of blocking and stage space, Marco and Maria's visit initiated the refinement process in the last week of practice before getting to the stage. This breath of fresh air, coming from such prominent yet unpretentious and truly helpful artists, was the subject of all of the students' successive journal entries, which, one-by-one, confirmed that that day, that encounter, and at that very point in our production, made for a profound and lasting memory.

III. FINAL REFLECTION

What happened between April 11 and April 13, 2009, in the Italian program at Indiana University? Several things: a unique learning experience about a specific time period in Italy and about an engaging and lesser-known theatrical genre; a unique opportunity to reflect as a faculty (professors and graduate students) about the evolution and current status of Italian theater today and to consider the places of monologue and historical dramas within them; a unique classroom experience for a group of undergraduates studying Italian theater; and an incredible human encounter for all.

The faculty and students at Indiana University were the very fortunate hosts of two major artists and two exceptional human beings. Onstage and off, Marco Baliani and Maria Maglietta were tapped into our experiences, our interests, and our questions. Their energy was contagious and throughout the visit, they were indefatigably accessible to us all. With their art and with their ways, they touched our lives and had a lasting impact on the entire community. They fueled our program with vivid examples of and personal reflections on theater as a literary genre, theater as an art and profession, and theater as a form of communication that reevaluates and proposes our (re)meditations on history.

Colleen Ryan
Department of French and Italian
Indiana University

Reviews: Wesleyan University, Performance at The Cinema, Middletown (April 16, 2009)

Body of State was a completely riveting and moving portrait of a man and an era that has stayed with me since we presented it at Wesleyan's Center for the Arts, April 16, 2009. It is important to note that at Wesleyan, we saw a very stripped-down production with slides and supertitles, just a suggestion of the technology used in the full production. This is important because our focus was all the more on Baliani, a single man on stage, telling us his story. As an actor and storyteller, Baliani has a unique ability to have everyone in the audience feel that he is telling the story only to them. . . . He doesn't have to try too hard to captivate. He has a commanding presence, a seductive voice, a dry humor and a very natural, conversational delivery that doesn't immediately let on to the powerhouse he becomes by the end of the piece. As an actor, he does not indulge the emotional undercurrent in the work, thereby enabling his audience to enter into that emotion in a far more personal and powerful way. I was particularly drawn into this work because my mother is a native Italian and, as a child, I had the great fortune of living in Milan in the early 1970s, the time that serves as the backdrop of Baliani's piece. Baliani drew me into the darker underbelly of that magnificent city that I had only known from a child's perspective. I understood the path of a person, an actor, who tasted the capacity of art to effect change in the world, and how he found his voice. I understood how he came to be drawn into the revolutionary zeal of his fellow compatriots. And most importantly, I understood the pain and confusion of a young man who, because of his rage against the corruption and discrimination of those in power, was tempted to use violence as a means to an end. The moment in the piece where he describes the riot that erupted, was when the work became most universal to me. I can still see that piazza; I see him lose his friend in the crowd. It was at that moment that Baliani became an "everyman" for me: a person who has ever believed in taking action against those in power and has had to struggle with how far they will go for what they believe in.

It was an honor to host this important work at the Center for the Arts and our students both of Theater and Italian were fortunate enough to meet with Baliani informally and to attend a workshop on his creative process. He is a generous, giving individual who has a great deal to impart to young people. We were lucky to have him in our midst.

Pamela Tatge
Center for the Arts
Wesleyan University

There were two bodies on stage that evening: Marco Baliani's living, breathing, speaking one, and Aldo Moro's corpse, ingrained in the collective mind as a photographic image of brutal death inside a car trunk. Between them stood Baliani's haunting performance—a text so powerful and its delivery so genuine—that it felt less like a theatrical piece and more like an attempt to give visual and auditory form to memory, that elusive world of lost fragments. Afterwards, I felt like I needed to know more not only about the dramatic events and the internally conflicted people that Baliani described, but also about these two men—one a tragic icon of a terrible moment in Italian history and the other a living reminder of that time, a voice of a generation that believed in higher ideals, but often struggled on how best to reach them. Baliani, it turns out, also writes fairy tales. Moro, too, seems to have been writing one with his "Historic Compromise."[1]

Two weeks before he was killed and his body found stuffed in the trunk of a red Renault 5 in the centre of Rome, there was a hoax communiqué that he was already dead and his corpse "submerged in the muddy waters of Lake Duchess" (May 1, 1978). But what the mountain troops fished out from that icy lake two days later was not Moro's iconic *Body of State*, but rather the body of a drowned shepherd, an unexpected supporting character in a pastoral tragedy about an Arcadia in which death was becoming commonplace and in which violent events of the present may have helped stage an almost more tragic future of corruption and indifference. Indeed, if Moro had lived to finish his tale, would the political landscape of Berlusconi's Italy look any different today? Every time Baliani as a shaman brings Moro's shadow back to his audiences, he raises questions not only about the past, but also about the present of Italy. The two moments are certainly very different, their main protagonists on the opposite ends of the political spectrum. But for both of them, I want to ask: how was that possible then, and how is this possible now? Sometimes these things, no matter how well we know them and from how many angles we analyze them, simply do not make any sense.

Nadja Aksamija
Department of Art and Art History
Wesleyan University

Watching Marco Baliani's *Body of State* in a half-filled, steeply-raked auditorium, with large English supertitles projected on a movie screen, was an intellectually intriguing but emotionally detached experience. The alienation effect produced by the titles and the setting distracted my attention from the performer and made his personal monologue seem like a lecture. Paradoxically, a video recording of the same performance conveyed a fuller sense of the intimacy of the piece and the urgency of its ethical content. Sitting at a laptop, watching a video in a language I only half understand, I was able to identify with Baliani's thoughts and feelings much more closely than I had in the live performance. Why? First, I think, because the video forced me to focus on Baliani's voice, body, and movement. Gone was the audience, gone the large, frequently changing supertitles demanding attention over the performer's head. What was left appeared to be the moving image of a man of roughly my age talking earnestly, passionately, to me, about experiences that shaped his life. The result was an illusion of intimacy that eluded me in the live performance. Second, in the video I was listening to Baliani's own language, and even though I didn't understand every word, I was able to hear the cadences and repetitions, to experience the rhetorical and emotional effect of his speech as well as the content of his stories. Against all expectation, the video conveyed a sense of intensity and immediacy that the setting and the trappings of the live but interpreted performance had obscured. Sharing the speaker's thoughts and emotions, especially his uncertainties about the relations of political ideologies, individual ambitions and motivations, personal loyalties and attachments, helped me understand the dilemmas he faced and the opposing principles he had to balance. Would acceding to the leaders' calls and the comrades' votes for *clandestinità* be an act of admirable political self-abnegation or a betrayal of essential political principle? Is his liminal position, *"né con le Brigate Rosse, né con lo stato"* (neither with the Red Brigades nor with the State), the result of a lack of conviction or a thoughtful and responsible consideration of the conditions on the ground and the principles at stake? The urgency of questions like these came across clearly in the video; watching it made me feel part of the piece's intended audience, charged to think seriously about the political problems it posed.

The live version, in contrast, raised different, equally compelling, questions about the nature, not the subject, of the performance. As an Italian audience would experience it, without titles, it would have been easy to believe that Baliani was recounting his youthful political activities and the personal significance of the Aldo Moro affair spontaneously, not for the first time, surely, but uniquely on this occasion, for this occasion, for us. He seemed at times to hesitate, to search for a word, to surprise himself with a memory, to be coming to terms with the painful past right there before our eyes. His actions, too, seemed spontaneous: a couple of dance steps, a shout, a bit of mimicry, seem ad-libbed, a charming part of this particular occasion. The titles, however, reminded us that none of this was true: the script was provided in advance, translated, projected. The timing was set. Baliani knew what he was going to say and do, and presumably what gestures and tones he would use, varying the detail as any actor must, but sticking to the script as translated. The illusion that he was speaking directly to us was precisely that, an illusion.

But all theatre is illusion, you might say. Helene Weigel is not Mother Courage; neither Cate Blanchett nor Hedda Gabler is dead at the end of the play. True, of course, but there's a difference here. Few theatre-goers confuse Weigel or Blanchett with the role she is playing or believe that Courage or Hedda is a real person. Baliani, in contrast, actually *is* Baliani. Or is he, and what exactly does this mean? At the beginning of the performance we are asked to welcome Marco Baliani. A man appears, nods to us, begins to speak. Surely this is Marco Baliani speaking to us. Well, it is and it isn't. This is the corporeal Marco Baliani assuming the voice, appropriating the language, and *pretending to be* the scripted Marco Baliani. Without the alienation effect of the titles, however, the audience is likely to take these two Balianis for one, and go home thinking that Marco Baliani has flown over from Italy, shared some thoughts and stories with us, answered a few questions, and is now enjoying a late-evening drink with the

Italian Department. In fact, the Marco Baliani who flew over from Italy, answered questions, and is now having drinks with Professor Nerenberg is related to the Marco Baliani of the performance as Cate Blanchett is related to Hedda Gabler. Cate flies over; Hedda shoots herself; Cate takes part in the talk-back and goes out for drinks afterward.

Body of State challenges dramatic convention by obscuring these distinctions. The titled performance foregrounded this challenge by making it impossible to ignore the scripted nature of the piece, and in the process raised questions about the ethics of performance. Is performing one's self inherently more deceptive than performing a character? If so, is this deception in some way dishonest, or just a somewhat more complicated version of the artifice involved in all forms of representation? Would it matter if Baliani's presentation had been introduced as an eyewitness account of a political era rather than a performance piece? These are questions that might be pertinent to performances by public figures of all sorts. What are Sarah Palin, Barack Obama, Rush Limbaugh, or Jon Stewart actually doing when they appear in public media? Speaking sincerely? Acting roles? Performing scripts? For me, the live performance of *Body of State* raised these questions even more forcefully than the ones contained in its own moving story.

William W. Stowe
Department of English
Wesleyan University

While driving down to Wesleyan University on the evening of April 16, 2009, to attend a performance of Marco Baliani's *Corpo di Stato: Il delitto Moro: Una generazione divisa* (*Body of the State: The Moro Affair, a Nation Divided*), I thought about those "years of lead" that culminated in the assassination of Aldo Moro. I was a junior in college deeply interested in all things Italian and followed the events on television and in the newspapers. When I arrived in Florence in the autumn of 1978 for my junior year abroad, several months after Moro's death, students I met at the university, people that befriended me, and mere acquaintances were still very shaken. To add to the national trauma, many of these people blamed Christian Democratic leaders because of their reluctance to negotiate Moro's release with the Red Brigades. For many critics, Andreotti, Cossiga and other officials had signed his death sentence. The chronology of events is well known, from the raid in via Fani in March to the discovery of Moro's corpse in a side street halfway between the Christian Democratic and the Communist Party's headquarters on May 9. But for all the "facts," there are still many unanswered questions. One thing is for sure: rather than destabilizing the State, the Red Brigades inadvertently solidified the ruling class's hold over civil society. With Moro's death, Italians of the late 1970s condemned armed violence as a means of radical political change. And in hindsight it perhaps marked a shift in Italians' hopes and attitudes toward even the idea that things could change at all. The aftershocks of "il caso Moro" were felt throughout the country for decades. And so, the Moro affair is worth retelling in the current political context, in which censorship, freedom of the press, and civil rights in Italy are again being challenged.

Thirty-one years have passed since the events narrated in *Body of State*, but Baliani's subjective and collective recollection made them eminently present. For the advanced level Italian students who came with me to the performance that evening and who only knew of Moro, the Red Brigades, the "years of lead" through Paul Ginsborg's historical writings, films such as Marco Tullio Giordana's *La meglio gioventù* (2003) and from course lectures, Baliani's piece is a popular eye-witness history of Italian politics and life in the 1970s.

The performance piece itself makes effective use of multimedia (music and black and white press images) that punctuate and complement the artist's monologue. But the piece's visuals and audio are like meaningful pauses in a dialogue, an opportunity to ponder the actor's words. Like all good storytellers, Baliani has a keen eye for detail, as in the tense incident about being stopped at a checkpoint by overly anxious young *carabinieri* with their machine guns raised. Who doesn't remember arriving at Rome's Fiumicino Airport or Termini train station in those days and for years afterward, and not seeing kids in uniform with machine guns! But Baliani's admission of fear during the checkpoint incident, his temporary paralysis, even his infant son's milk bottle rolling into the gutter are all the bizarre details of his traumatic experience. They are precisely the kinds of things we remember forever. And like a popular poet, Baliani deftly mimics the different voices and linguistic registers, from militants' hackneyed political slogans to expressions of shock among people on the street.

A key moment in the performance piece comes early when Baliani parallels Moro's kidnapping in Rome with Giuseppe Impastato's brutal murder in Sicily at the hands of the Mafia. Impastato was a journalist and radio host who denounced the Mafia over the airways. Beaten to a pulp by several henchmen, Impastato was then sheathed in dynamite and detonated. This horrid and gruesome image as recounted by Baliani is juxtaposed with Moro's contorted and bullet-riddled body in the trunk of a red Renault casually parked in via Caetani. The crimes are not directly related per se but the parallel is enough to remind us of the ties between the State, Mafia (and Camorra), and political terrorism.

Baliani's monologue works as art, not only because of its insight about Italy's collective consciousness, namely that outside of armed insurrection, there was little or no room for open discourse in the face of government censorship and repression, but because of the artist's talent for moving in and out of voice(s) and because he weaves standard narrative and personal memories with those of bystanders and fellow Italians. There are dramatic anecdotes about violent protests gone really bad, about young friends who inadvertently become martyrs to the radical movement, or about political fellow travelers who do hard time in jail because they hide arms for militants out of peer pressure. In the end, Baliani wistfully reflects: "We all came from the same great dream" ("Venivamo tutti dallo stesso grande sogno"). Given the current Italian political context, the dream of social and political justice that many thought was within reach in the 1970s paradoxically seems even further away today. As I write this review (early October 2009), public protests are being held in several major European cities and throughout Italy in defense of freedom of the press. The Italian State's reaction to Moro's tragic death was to clamp down on civil rights in the name of public order. Just as the protest movement of the 1960s and 1970s was a reaction to authoritarian rule of the first half of the 20th century, perhaps the current debate in Italy over freedom of the press and other civil rights issues (including immigrants' rights) is the attempt to reverse a political trend in Italian civil society that seems to have begun in the aftermath of Moro's assassination. Whether this is Baliani's intention for performing his play today matters little. The point may be that we *all* continue to come from the same great dream.

Dario Del Puppo
Department of Languages and Cultural Studies
Trinity College, Hartford

On Theater Travels and Translations: Body of State goes to Wesleyan University

The notion of the theater as a threshold that differentiates as it conjoins a whole range of seemingly oppositional realms (Michal Kobialka, "Introduction," *Of Borders and Thresholds: Theater History, Practice and Theory* [Minneapolis: University of Minnesota Press, 1999]) offers a suggestive point of departure for reflecting on Marco Baliani's recent presentation of *Body of State* in Middletown, Connecticut. I refer here not to *Body of State* in and of itself, understood in its more or less conventional format as a stage production, but rather to Baliani in Middletown as a theater event in the broadest sense, with various layers of significance transecting his peripheral, pre- and post-production interventions that were essentially pedagogical, that were held in different venues (lounges, homes), and that converged in the transnationalized/supertitled *Body of State* as presented on stage at Wesleyan University's Center for the Arts on May 16, 2009, between 8 p.m. and 9 p.m. The prime vector within this multi-dimensional schema corresponds to the image of Baliani as pilgrim progressing on stage toward an epiphany: toward a deeper understanding of the inter-relatedness of self and society, individual and nation; toward what proves to be an illusive reconciliation between a past fraught with pain for those who, like Baliani, dared to dream, and a present at odds with such dreams as it is dominated (as Baliani *glossed* during the Q & A and *showed* on stage) by either the ghosts of 1968 or citizens blind to such ghosts. Baliani crusades relentlessly both to teach the blind to see and to be seen. The theater becomes his *liminoid* (per Victor Turner and Richard Schechner) threshold—theater "saved me," he insists, and we are to presume that it does so with each new performance—where deep level realizations occur. Suspended in time and disconnected from the material world that it interrogates, Baliani's theater becomes the moment and place where the links between seemingly oppositional zones of experience (places, times, identities) are unveiled, where phantasmagoria are materialized.

The most stunning correlation has to do with the confusion and violence that Baliani attributes to the "then" on the national plane and that endures in the "now" of his intimate domain. Such a correlation can take shape only through the act of telling. The mythical matrix of his mental wanderings remains close to the surface of his telling as he meanders through the "selva oscura" [dark wood] of his memories seeking understanding, reconciliation, and peace, by means of the tools of his trade, the words and gestures with which he articulates what is for him the haunting link (chaos, fear) between past and future:

> Baliani: "che *stava succedendo* dentro di me . . . è ancora difficile parlarne dopo tanti anni . . ."
>
> Dante: "Ahi quanto a dir qual *era è* cosa dura . . ."
>
> [Baliani: What was happening inside of me . . . it's still difficult to talk about after many years.
>
> Dante: How difficult it was and is to say . . .]

The cadence and content of his telling contain the road marks of a quest for meaning that, as it becomes increasingly apparent, adheres to the mythical pattern of a descent: into the quagmire of unanswered questions ("what were we to do?"), into the horrors of Moro's 55-day *passion*, and toward the connection Baliani brings into focus between the Calvary of his own telling and the specter of an empty coffin at Moro's state funeral. Baliani's post-production Q & A gloss on this historical event is intrinsic to his Middletown performance, since it allows his American audience to grasp the semiotics of his telling. The equation that emerges between two static images, the empty coffin is likened to the empty state since both are devoid of their "corpi," or bodies ("di Moro," "di stato") is ultimately subsumed by the dominant and dynamic projection of the very act of divesting the iconic coffin of its substance. The prime agents of this travesty, Andreotti and Paul VI, become the producers and protagonists of the banal farce that replays endlessly, embedded as it is in the imagination of the "corpo"

(Baliani's) that, in the end, reigns supreme (semiotically speaking). In this spectacle of lost hopes and failed accomplishments, Baliani constructs himself as the composite social "corpo" of the children of '68, divested, like him, of their past dreams. We are left, paradoxically, with the image of a void in the making. In the final analysis, Baliani's monologue is a postmortem for self, society, and the state in the postmodern era in which the dogma of "solidarity" and "social justice" (Baliani) are brutally relativized as empty reminders of an axial order.

Of course, performance gains meaning only through a semiosis that is realized immediately and collectively by the audience, especially in a work like Baliani's *Body of State* given the speaker's emphasis on direct discourse and gestures that beckon his interlocutors (spectators) to enter his intimate domain. This brought me to ponder the reach of this work's messianic overtones the night of the stage production. The experience of seeing an actor proffering himself up as martyr on the altar of contemporary culture must be disconcerting at the very least for those who either ignore or deny any need for redemption. In the same vein I was left wondering how the supertitles might deter from the Dionysian scheme of Baliani's experience. It seems that the didacticism that pervaded Baliani's Wesleyan performance and that issues to some degree from its context might trump the desired pathos and thereby divest his performance of the richness of its essential paradox, making it a threshold that divides without conjoining. It is clear, however, that Wesleyan/academic context is not the only such impediment, given Baliani's reference in his post-stage production commentary to the many young Italians in need of supertitles of a different kind, in non-academic settings. A perplexing thought indeed, considering the stakes involved. The tragic loss of historical memory (a pre-stage production topic for discussion): yet another empty coffin, "corpo di stato," threshold that fissures.

Such considerations would apply, of course, in any *transnationalized* psychosocial drama predicated, as is Baliani's, on the interrelatedness of self and society in times of crisis. "I represent the nation"—Baliani tells us obliquely—"and I am here to give personal testimony to our collective trauma hoping to facilitate some degree of social reconciliation." That is: the "theater saved me and it can now save us." The processual scope of this collectivized pilgrim's progress unifies *Body of State* much as it does the performances of Eduardo Pavlovsky, the Argentinean actor-playwright and psychotherapist who has essayed widely on the therapeutic nature of the stage. Whereas Baliani aims directly for the heart, Pavlovsky jolts his compatriots toward recovery *alienatedly* (Brecht) by representing the heinous inner world of the torturer (*El señor Galíndez*) or his accomplice (*Potestad*). My personal experience with *Potestad* offers an intriguing case in point. The borders that Pavlovsky crossed to represent, in Madrid, the doctor who, in a post-military/democratic Argentina, progresses in his own telling toward a riveting confession of his military-era sins (he sanctioned the kidnapping of children of executed leftists) were all circumscribed in the Madrid performance by a language common to the performer and his audience (Spanish), the differences of dialect and national experience notwithstanding. More importantly, the performance was held in a small neighborhood theater, with a number of South American refugees in attendance. Pavlovsky was blessed with interlocutors who already shared his intimacy to some degree and who were prepared to feel the full effect of the criminal's problematic contrition, of the pathos vying to displace our sense of repugnance.

In *Potestad* the drama hinges on the moment of the character's confession, when Pavlovsky suddenly finds himself dripping in the blood of his victims (the squirt gun is hidden in the flies). A correlation might exist between this scene and the pivotal moment in *Body of State* when the character Marco Baliani, another victim-agent of history and nationhood, acknowledges the profound shame he felt—"mi alzai con un senso di vergogna addosso" [I got up feeling a sense of shame]—resulting from the clandestine antics of his erstwhile companions, a shame that left him mute—"senza parole" [without words], tragically divested of the tools of his trade—and that leaves the audience questioning the thorny ethics of Italian politics and movements of the 1970s. Pavlovsky's communion with his audience, as evidenced by the sobs of some and the tense silence of many, is a response to be imagined in a *Body of State* presented without the pedagogical framework, as pure or "poor" (Grotowski) theater, in a small theater in a working-class neighborhood, perhaps, in Rome, Milan, or Turin. As a pedagogue and theater scholar I am left hoping that Baliani's Wesleyan audience derived a richer and deeper understanding of how essential their own role is in the construction of meaning in performance.

Bernardo Antonio González
Department of Romance Languages and Literatures
Wesleyan University

Reviews and Student Responses: Dickinson College, Performance at the *Cubiculo* and Residency, Carlisle (April 21–24, 2009)

LOOKING AT THEM LOOKING: TEACHERS' REFLECTIONS

"Where Were You When They Kidnapped Aldo Moro?"

In the pre-performance discussion with students at Dickinson College (April 21, 2009), Marco Baliani and Maria Maglietta shared their memories about the making of *Body of State*. Marco was bewildered by RAI's proposal; he never thought he could be a candidate for this job, since he took part in the Student Movement in the 1970s, and certainly, he would have not delivered a conventionally commemorative speech. Marco and Maria ventured into this project accompanied by a group of other collaborators. For my students, it was unusual and difficult to grasp how his solo performance will not be a "monologue." His one voice was going to tell the stories of the many he had met, worked with, and talked to. But he would also play the role of those against whom they had fought, such as the Mafia boss who killed Peppino Impastato. Marco explained that practically, suddenly bursting in the middle of the conversation and saying, changing inflection, with a Sicilian accent: "intellettuale, cornuto, comunista!" [intellectual, cuckold, and communist].

After a long period of researching and investigating the documents about Aldo Moro's kidnapping and death, together with his group, Marco could not find a conclusion. He felt, at some point, that their efforts were in vain. How could they create a show without falling into a repetition of what has been already said, many and many times, by endless news reports and books and essays? Things changed suddenly when Maria posed a question: "Where were you when they kidnapped Aldo Moro?"

Reading *Body of State*, before they met Marco, my students highlighted the intertwining of public and private memories, and were especially struck by the recollection of friends' involvement (more or less directly) in the terrorist guerrilla organizations. In the pre-performance discussion, we discovered the shift from the supposedly objective historical research to the subjective experiences of the event constituted the actual genesis of *Body of State*. Furthermore, we gathered that the perspective from which the authors would look at their project had changed, throughout, from the "what we know" to the "where we were." Maria's question made me think about the relationship between space and time, vis-à-vis the audience and the actor, in the moment of the performance. In order to make sense of a past that they intended to narrate, the actors (meaning not only the performer but all involved/acting in the making of the story) moved from the present of the documents, which they were reading, to the past of their own memories. This motion consisted in a recollection by/of their bodies: Where were you? How did you feel? What did you do?

When the Red Brigades kidnapped and killed Aldo Moro, my students of Italian Literature at Dickinson College were not yet born. When Moro's death was commemorated year after year, my students were thousands of miles away, both physically and figuratively. Preparing them for Marco and Maria's visit, I wondered if they were going to be able to engage with them in a thoughtful conversation and how I could help them have a meaningful experience of the performance. Part of my work then was to provide students with a background on the historical, social and political context. Above all, I saw as crucial to highlight the issues at stake when one narrates the past: the "uses and abuses of history," in Nietzsche's words, and the relationship between subjective experiences and historical narratives. I thought, at that time, that I could substitute knowledge and intellectual debate for the physical and cultural belonging that American students lacked. My students, on the other hand, carried a genuine curiosity about "Signor Baliani," an actor from Italy who will be doing some out-of-the-ordinary mise-en-scène in the Cubicle where, just a few months before, many of them performed a play by Dario Fo to a friendly audience of family and friends. Will they be as friendly, I asked myself, as their own audience?

In my view, sharing his initial impasse with us, Marco demonstrated that at the origins of *Body of State* was not so much the need to produce something original, but rather, the will to create something meaningful, both for them and for the audience. Hayden White has written that historical narratives constitute the way in which cultures can make sense of themselves. It seems to me that *Body of State* is the attempt of the generation who has lived through the Movement in the 1970s to make sense of itself, through storytelling. *Body of State* tells about Moro's kidnap and death as the event that signed this generation's suicidal death.

In their responses to the performance, my students emphasized how they were moved, excited, surprised, and sometimes distressed, "forgetting" that the play was in Italian and completely drawn to the happening scene. The black box of the solo-actor space where Baliani performed (the *Cubiculo*), I thought, contributed to create the intimacy between the speaker and the spectators, while the screens projecting scenes of riots further mobilized their physical and emotional reactions. Both the actor and the audience were there, in the same place: Carlisle, 2009. At the same time, both the actor and the audience inhabited the space/time of narration: Italy, 1978. The past and the present happening simultaneously, time realized as duration. In such duration, we would bridge the unbridgeable differences, empathizing with a generation that disappeared long ago. We felt injustice—Marco made us feel—for the sudden death of his friend Giorgio, stupidly trying to show his braveness to the Red Brigades; for the murderous death of Peppino Impastato, fighting against the Mafia; for the suicidal death of the Student Movement, stuck in between a repressive State and a criminal organization. Carrying these feelings in our own bodies, it will be up to us to make justice (me, my students, anyone at the show), in our own time and the many spaces we will live in.

Paola Bonifazio
Department of French and Italian
University of Texas, Austin

The afternoon before seeing Marco Baliani's performance *Body of State: The Moro Affair, a Nation Divided* at Dickinson College, I brought the students in my senior seminar in French Theatre to speak with Baliani in the black box studio theatre where he was rehearsing for the evening's show. Baliani talked to us about his work and shared some video clips from his 1994 performance *Come gocce di una fiumana* (*Like Drops in a Human River*). For the show he worked with texts taken from letters exchanged between First World War soldiers and their families. The highly physical performance was staged outdoors, in the courtyard of what looked like a fortress, with audience members all around the many performers who embodied the pain and sorrow brought on by the separation caused by war. Our conversation was particularly interesting because it showed the students how texts not intended for performance can be brought to life. Baliani graciously responded to the students' questions and clarified his approach to space, to relating text and performance, and to helping actors bring their whole beings to the creative process. He shared his vision of theatre that connects politics and personal experience.

After seeing clips of large groups of performers in a vast space in *Come gocce di una fiumana*, seeing *Body of State* was all the more remarkable for its simple staging. On stage the two video screens were placed on either side of the stage, and between them was a metal-framed cube serving as a chair. In his costume, a dark brown jacket, a brown dress shirt, dark grey pants, he looked almost like a professor.

Near the beginning of the play, Baliani talked about being a student and creating theatre with Dario Fo. He said they were creating "raw, simple, deeply political theatre." He put his faith in words instead of weapons, and his thoughtfulness on stage inspires us to stop and reflect rather than simply react. This is political theater for dialogue rather than for dogma. One man on a stage, talking to the audience is as simple as theatre can get.

Though many in the audience had to follow the subtitles to understand the words, Baliani's physical and vocal presence communicated so much. With his bare hands, Baliani evokes weapons and murder: he raises his hand into the air like a gun, pointing it at the audience; he holds an imaginary club and counts the blows inflicted on a protestor by police; he throws an invisible Molotov cocktail; he cradles the weight of a gun wrapped in newspaper in a plastic bag. In this raw theatre, words and gestures make violence real enough for the audience to share in Baliani's aversion to it as a means of creating revolutionary change. His tone is often conversational, he pauses to think, and to search for words. He is capable of stillness, silence and waiting. The subtitle screens wait too, so all of us, regardless of language, can hold a breath, wait, think, pause . . . exhale and go on again, further into the personal impact of the events recounted in the play.

When Baliani first mentions "bellissima Sara," or gorgeous Sara, in the context of a political meeting, his body language, including a goofy double thumbs up gesture as he sits next to her, elicits some of the loudest general laughter of the night. It is a good moment of comic relief and a reminder to many of the students that some motives for participating in political action are not always lofty and intellectual.

When Baliani discusses what he would do were "gorgeous Sara" to knock on his door one night, looking for a place to stay, his body language is fabulous. He indicates a line in front of him, the doorway, ushering her in by sweeping his right arm back and turning as though letting her pass, then stepping forward and putting up his right hand as if to say "Stop." He vacillates on this imaginary line, beautifully illustrating the sad and confusing tension of being "neither here nor there." It is so hard to choose sides, wanting to preserve oneself, one's family, and also not wanting to condemn old friends from political groups to arrest or death. In this moment, though the audience was quiet, his honest inner conflict resonated.

What moved and impressed me about Baliani's performance was the personal way in which he recounted his youthful idealism and his involvement in various political organizations in the years leading up to 1978. He told the stories of his friends with whom he initially shared ideological viewpoints, and how as his friends became increasingly radical, he chose not to follow them in their violent exploits. As I watched the performance, I wondered how the students from Dickinson and the other colleges who had joined us in the room were reacting to the story. Before this night, how many of these audience members in central Pennsylvania knew anything about the kidnapping of Aldo Moro by the Red Brigades? He was talking about a kind of unfamiliar, radical political activity from another era and another country.

The attraction to radical political activity, the call to violence in the name of "revolution" seems like something to which the students with whom I sat could not relate. I sensed they didn't really understand the impassioned call to arms, even though they might want to change the world. Over 30 years after 1978, I'm not sure the students in the theatre really understood the importance of that date. However, the fact that Baliani was a young person himself at the time of the Moro kidnapping made the play well suited to the audience of which I was a part. The great gift of Marco Baliani's *Body of State* is that it makes the personal political and the political personal.

Ian Andrew MacDonald
Department of French and Italian
Dickinson College

Looking at Them Looking: Notes on Dickinson Students' Reception
of Body of State

Marco Baliani's three-day event at Dickinson College was amazing for its discussions, performances, screenings, and, above all, for its enthusiastic reception by students of Italian.

The students were introduced to the theatrical performance by a discussion with Baliani and were given the opportunity to comment on the performance the day after during the post-performance discussion. Most students were not aware of Italian history after WWII and did not realize how difficult the "years of lead" were, when terrorism was at its height. Thus, the air taken out of many stereotypes about Italy and Italians and Italy was seen with a different perspective. Students' idea of Italy just as a food-style-arts region changed into a more accurate vision of a country shaken and still suffering because of the controversial experiences of the 1970s. In particular, students appreciated the fact that Baliani was talking about his personal experience. In fact, during the pre- and post-performance discussions, it was made clear that he was not only the narrator, the author and the actor, but also a live witness of dramatic events whose consequences affect today's Italian society. 18-year-old minds were impressed by Baliani's travelling around the States as if he was a "wayfarer," exposing his private history inserted in the social history. They discovered the importance of being an active part in society even if this can lead to moral crises and problematic decisions.

Also, students enjoyed their general understanding of the play and looked at the supertitles only every now and then. The strong emotiveness of the performance, together with Baliani's skillful ability to communicate his feelings through movements, gestures, yelling, whispers, pauses and silences, provoked attentive listening and visual perception. Complicated words to translate, such as "Movimento" [Student Movement], "anni di piombo" ["years of lead," when terrorism was at its height], "compagno" [comrade], "carabiniere" [Italian police force, which is a branch of the army], "Democrazia Cristiana" [Christian Democratic Party], and "Brigate Rosse" [Red Brigades], became immediately understandable and acquired the potency of key words able to open the door of history.

As an instructor, watching Dickinson students view *Body of State* was an enlightening experience. Immersed in the dark scenario and in a deep silence, their shining, questioning eyes wide open to grab every detail, they became part of the performance, highlighting its real purpose—to function not as a monologue but as a dialogue.

Adele Sanna
Department of Romance Languages
University of Virginia

STUDENTS' RESPONSES: EXTRACTS FROM JOURNALS AND BLOGS

Body of State: *A New Perspective*

Prior to reading *Body of State*, I viewed the Red Brigades as merely a fringe terrorist group. After learning more details about the Moro kidnapping and the fact that the whole story surrounding the events is still unclear, I am slightly less harsh in my judgment of them. Although I am still absolutely opposed to the kidnapping and murder of an elected official as a political gesture, *Body of State* made the context of the time period more apparent, and I can better understand why these groups behaved in the way that they did. I was unaware of how violent this era was in Italian history. The implementation of the "Legge Reale," which gave police the right to kill individuals that they deemed to be dangerous, is one example of this escalation of violence.[2] In response, some of those who were treated wrongfully by the police took up arms against them. This cycle of escalation and retaliation seems to me to be key for understanding why people were so angry and militant; once violence is introduced into a situation, it is difficult to return to a nonviolent state. Although the 60s were also a violent decade in the United States, the level and overall scope of the violence throughout the country seems to have been much less pronounced than that of Italy. I think that the firsthand accounts of this time period in *Body of State* made the events much more relatable to the audience.

Genevieve Saul
Dickinson College, Class of 2009

A Theater of Conflict

It is profound to learn that Baliani's love for theatre began not from a typical exposure to acting or cinema, but rather from conflict. It seems as though theatre was an escape for Baliani; a place for him to transform into someone else and escape from the trials and tribulations of his adolescence in Italy between the 1960s and 1970s.

During the discussions with Baliani, before and after performing *Body of State*, he stressed that his works were not typical works of theatre. Baliani centered his life around the art of memory; recounting his life by way of theatre and acting. Baliani's work is not a monologue, but rather the recitation of memory. In Baliani's performance, it was difficult to understand where art and reality began and ended. Baliani seemed to be providing descriptions of images which the audience was to create in their minds, rather than actually seeing Baliani creating these portrayals. Baliani's stage presence was captivating; however, it was not overbearing, thus allowing the audience to create their own impressions and images of Baliani's memories.

Zoe Lutz
Dickinson College, Class of 2012

Monologue vis-à-vis Narration

Baliani made a clear distinction between monologue and narration. I was unaware of this distinction, so his explanation was very helpful. He stated that *Body of State* was not a monologue because it engaged the audience, which he believed was more advantageous for both him and the audience. To start a narration, Baliani believes that you need someone to ask you the right questions, otherwise you will not be able to collect the right information that is essential to give life to a play or book. Additionally, he stated that theatre does not explain, it asks questions. He believes that if the audience walks away without a sense of shock or inquiry, then the narrator has not done a good job of recounting his story.

Chiara Olivi
Dickinson College, Class of 2011

Q & A with Baliani

Since we had read a chapter from Baliani's *Body of State* the week before his presentation, as a class we were made familiar with his vision as an author and as an actor. The question and answer session the night before the presentation also allowed us to ask questions and hear more about his personal history and his creative process before seeing all of his hard work performed. I enjoyed having a separation between the question and answer period and the presentation itself—giving us time to reflect on his statements and explanations to our questions before viewing his show.

From my previous classes, I knew about the *strategia della tensione* but did not fully understand what it meant for the common, everyday Italian, even if they had not personally been affected by any of the large tragedies: Piazza Fontana, Bologna Centrale, etc.[3] Baliani's physical presentation with its audio-visual projections on the wall helped me to further understand the situation in Italy in ways that merely reading his work did not.

Allyson Glazier
Dickinson College, Class of 2011

The Perception of Truth

Baliani's memoir is thought-provoking because like much of Italian theater and literature, the aim of the work is not truth, but perception. Baliani mentioned this during the pre-performance discussion in which he stated that theater is meant to show conflict, not explain things; there is no truth. The effect of this technique is rather profound because, in a sense, it gives a more accurate representation of the social tension at the time and a personal insight into the reactions of the public to Moro's kidnapping as well as the advent of violence and extra-parliamentary political groups. Interestingly, this quality is repeated in Bellocchio's *Buongiorno, notte* (2003), where Chiara, a fictional character playing the part of one of Moro's kidnappers, struggles with her affiliation with the Brigate Rosse as she recognizes that her actions mirror those of the fascists that killed her father, a partigiano, years before.

The other unique quality of Baliani's representation is the importance of improvisation in storytelling. As Baliani mentioned in our discussion, "Non si scrive prima . . . si scrive dopo" [you don't write before but afterward]. This dynamic creates an interesting dimension to the work because it is raw, it is flawed, it is uncensored, it is unfinished, and it is unadorned with thoughtful refinements. When speaking directly from experience to a live audience, there is no time to edit one's words, to restate things, or to monitor what is said. There is only time to feel and re-experience, and in doing so present the audience with a time-capsule simulation, in this case, of the omnipresent social tension that characterized this tumultuous period in Italian history.

Sharon Perrone
Dickinson College, Class of 2011

Timing and Movement

In our post-performance discussion we talked about the power of timing in theater. Baliani gave a few examples where he said the same sentence but with different timings, he noted how each timing gave different implications to the sentence and that a good actor must know how to employ this method. We also talked about the movements of an actor and their effect on the audience. Baliani showed us a clip of one of his performances where he remained seated the entire time. While narrating the story, Baliani would often show strong emotions and would make it appear like he would get up from the chair, but he never did. His remaining seated had a large effect on the audience; it created a type of tension in the theater. It became clear that Baliani had employed both of these techniques during his performance at Dickinson, and that without them the performance would not have the same flair.

Elena Brandano
Dickinson College, Class of 2011

Crossing Barriers

Especially to an American student, *Body of State* helps bring to life and make real the political situation and its effect on society during the time of the kidnapping of Moro. Currently in the United States, even with the recent major election of President Barack Obama, college students and young adults in general are not as politically conscious or passionate as those in Italy during that time period. It is hard for a student like myself to imagine and try to understand the feelings like those of Marco Baliani, who was part of active extra-parliamentary groups. The idea seems very foreign to me. *Body of State*, which gives you the viewpoint and feelings of a person during that time which they lived through, is very effective in crossing this barrier and creating a level of understanding for the reader or spectator.

During one of the discussion times with Marco Baliani, a student asked about his current thoughts on a particular event from *Body of State*. He said that he now would feel differently about the situation, which to me seems natural since 30 years have gone by and the current situation (in Italy and personally for Marco Baliani) is very different. However, when telling us this, Baliani emphasized the importance of not transmitting his current sentiments during the performance of *Body of State*, but how he felt then.

Kelly Zwink
Dickinson College, Class of 2009

Acting as a Way of Being

Acting is not easy and it is a way of being. I like how he interpreted *Body of State* through his gestures. I was also impressed by the accuracy of the subtitles. We really understood how people acted in the 1970s. Marco Baliani also made me think of Dario Fo because he was so focused on what he was talking about. I think that someone who is able to act in such a way cannot be considered an artist because acting is a job. Baliani lived through the "years of lead" and Moro's kidnapping, and he really made me feel as if I was living those years too.

Luciano Di Palermo
Dickinson College, Class of 2009

Not Like a Movie

When I saw him performing I realized his aim was not to entertain people but to teach them something. He used many stylistic features while performing. I particularly liked how he stood in the light because it gave the idea that it was his story he was telling, Marco's story, from his unique perspective. Moreover, he used a combination of language and images. This turned out to be very effective because the videos showed the past events, while the language was a means to express his emotions and share his memories.

Marco explained his perspective of the images, which is very important since the story consists of many perspectives, not only facts. This is similar to the representation of the Holocaust in cinema and books because artists and actors can represent something new, just as Marco did. Another stylistic feature was his tone. During the discussion, he said his tone was normal, not too dramatic because he didn't want to romanticize his story and turn it into a Hollywood movie. As in a movie about the Holocaust, his tone was very important because it adds to the message.

Brian Krusell
Dickinson College, Class of 2011

He Brought Silent Stories to Life

I found it very interesting what he told us about the social tension between neighbors and friends because it reminded me of the tensions between fascists and Jews during the Holocaust. I also thought about *The Garden of the Finzi-Continis* (1970) because in this movie/book friends turn into foes and you can understand how the structure of the government changed after a serious incident. I also liked that Marco wanted to tell his story to Americans because I think we should learn from the past. Marco is also a good actor. He was able to change roles quickly. The lack of a set design helped the audience to concentrate on the character and not the background. It is significant that Baliani chose theatre instead of television or cinema as a means to tell his story because the lack of special effects makes us focus more on the story itself and the emotions. Marco was able to bring silent stories to life.

Perrin Allen
Dickinson College, Class of 2011

From Different Perspectives

The images reproduced on stage are effective because they express the sense of fragmentation and division between Marco's two different perspectives on

Aldo Moro's kidnapping and the Red Brigades. The staggering of the scenes provided a time for both audience and Marco to reflect on the events of the play, which proved moving and effective. He also proved through the use of gestures how problems caused by miscommunication can be overcome through body language.

Michael Dalton
Dickinson College, Class of 2009

A Vivid Story

It was great to meet Marco Baliani and see him performing. His play, *Body of State*, was simple yet effective. I could actually picture the story he was telling. I also think that his personal story intertwines with the historical events of the 1970s in Italy. *Body of State* is similar to many representations of the Holocaust we saw, where characters' micro-stories tell us about a macro-story. The theater of narration is very effective because the audience can imagine and picture what the actor is trying to express. In this way the story is more vivid.

Lucie Carrara
Université Toulouse Le Mirail, Class of 2010

Marco and Primo

We already knew the "official" story of the violence in the 1970s as well as Aldo Moro's assassination but listening to these accounts from Baliani's perspective makes them seem more real and accessible. His method is similar to that employed by Primo Levi in his book *Survival in Auschwitz*. Like Levi, Baliani conveys a story by describing important characters and then asking us to imagine something we had never thought about, something he saw and experienced but that we wouldn't be able to understand without his guidance and logic. His method is to paint a picture of something that his audience will find familiar, thus providing a useful starting point from which he introduces changes, nuances, and details that bring his viewers into his world. It is a simple yet effective method of helping his audience gain a clearer picture of what he has heard and seen.

Brendan Stuart
Dickinson College, Class of 2009

Reviews: Northwestern University, Performance at McCormick Tribune Center Forum, Chicago (May 4, 2009)

Marco Baliani's Body of State*: Growing with the Story*

The touring performance by Marco Baliani, *Body of State: The Moro Affair* (*Corpo di Stato*, Rizzoli, 2003), came to Northwestern on May 4, 2009, sponsored by the Department of Italian and the Istituto Italiano di Cultura in Chicago.

The Italian faculty had talked a lot about that event and tried to think of effective ways to present the subject matter to the undergraduates. How could we engage the students with a period of Italian history so peculiar and complex? We had submitted the Italian curriculum for the current academic year long before the initiative of inviting Baliani took shape. Thus there was neither space nor time to design *ad hoc* classes, targeting language proficiency while presenting content. Thanks to the flexibility of some programs (and instructors), however, quite a few classes—second year and intensive Italian—were able to incorporate *Body of State* (or at least some excerpts) into their reading assignments. Nevertheless, in order to shed light on the historical and political complexity of Italy in the 1970s and contextualize Baliani's work, we had to expose students to additional material. We therefore developed a broad variety of extra-curricular activities, among which were the screening of some documentaries from the archive of RAI Educational and two films, *I cento passi* (2000) and *Buongiorno, notte*. In order to foster a student-centered approach and increase motivation, instructors operated as facilitators, assigning undergraduates to do research on the "anni di piombo" and "terrorismo rosso e nero," individually or in small groups, and then to share findings with peers and faculty. Informal conversations (rather than formal lectures) took place and students, in addition to gathering information, were able to exchange opinions and insights, to ask and answer questions.

Had they really learned anything in terms of Italian culture? I would say yes, they had. Being exposed to authentic materials and different media, being confronted with complex information, and playing an active role in constructing the historical and political background certainly motivated students to retain information that could help them contextualize Aldo Moro's kidnapping and assassination. However, the cognitive process achieved its completeness only during Marco Baliani's performance, when the students could engage emotionally. Suddenly the material we had supplied them became alive. Only then, in fact, did the content turn meaningful to them.

Italy's social and political situation in the 1970s could be complex even for those who lived there, let alone for someone—like the students—who was born in recent years and has known the word terrorism in a deeply different historical and political context. How could such a difficult message be properly contextualized, conveyed, and made clear? The answer to this question lies in Marco Baliani's performance. Not only was a chapter of Italian history illuminated on stage, but the story of a man was unveiled. Questions, memories, doubts, personal reflections flowed and created a silent dialogue between the protagonist and the audience. The actor disappeared, the script vanished and the man seemed to be left alone with his inner struggle and his vulnerability. The tone of voice was calm, the rhythm of speech slow. He paused frequently, searching—his memory, his heart, his soul?—for the most faithful and precise words to express his feelings, recount his experience, his past, the past of his generation, and the past of his country. He was thinking aloud, trying to shape definitive words, to find definitive answers. He sat down, stood up, walked back and forth, perhaps seeking in motion what he could not find verbally. Yet the sense of restlessness and discomfort could not be soothed. A need to understand and reconcile ideals and dreams with justice and responsibility would continue to torment him and reiterate the same questions. There was neither anger nor resignation, neither regret nor remorse, neither reproach nor approval. Like a ghost appearing from the dark came the echo of the incessant question to which there is no answer: What if things had gone differently? Yet there was no attempt to cloud the past, rather a profound need to understand both the historical and political scenario and himself, and to find out whether he was able to respect the Pindaric admonition "become what you are."

This way, Marco Baliani not only brought history to life, but connected past to present through the thread of his humanity and the progression—with no few difficulties—of his own life. By making human—and consequently relevant to young adults coming from a different cultural background—a perspective that could otherwise be received as just another class assignment, Baliani was able to draw the audience into the flow of his thoughts, stir curiosity, motivate and inspire self-reflection. Students could empathize with the man and engage emotionally. *Mutatis mutandis*, I believe that they were able to relate to the account and the lived experience that Baliani was sharing with them, feel its intensity, and grasp the distress. Encouraged to reflect on their own cultural and historical context and to think of their personal story and experience, they could appreciate intercultural and generational differences. Furthermore, watching and connecting with a man who does not want to be a hero and keeps analyzing and questioning his actions as a way to be alive and loyal to himself let students learn a piece of authentic human life, so authentic and so human because full of both courage and fear.

Paola Morgavi
Department of French and Italian
Northwestern University

Marco Baliani in Body of State*: The Story of Our Stories*

I am sitting in the audience of McCormick Tribune Forum at Northwestern University. The set is limited to the bare essentials, a chair, a screen and nothing more. The lights in the auditorium are dimmed, and the spotlight takes Marco Baliani out of the shadow. It is the start of a *dramatic* journey. Another world comes to life through Baliani's words.

From 2009 we are instantly projected back to 1978, to the days of the kidnapping and killing of Aldo Moro. But this is neither a historical analysis nor a political reading of that episode; it is the story of our stories, the ones who were there at that time, at that age. It is the story of the mixed whirl of dreams and fears that we first lived and then tried to forget. The character on stage is not simply a narrator, he is a powerful catalyst: all the questions—born back at that time and still unanswered—come back to my mind while his voice peels off the layers of my willful forgetfulness.

The tone of the narration is introspective, almost confidential. The bareness of the stage and the shadows allow the immediate flow of emotions from the narrator to the audience. Marco Baliani exposes his feelings, his fears, and his doubts, mixing them with simple daily stories from his memory of those times.

The image of Aldo Moro and his dead body hovers as a presence over the audience all the time. Through authentic media excerpts from the news of the period, which flow in short flashes on the screen behind the narrator, History enters the stories. But then the stories shape History when Marco Baliani revives on stage details, emotions, atmospheres, inner conflicts, delusion, and disillusionment.

Marco Baliani is wonderful at alternating the two levels of the narration, being neither too detached nor over-passionate. The unique strength of his narration lies in his ability to mix facts and emotions, high concepts and details. As in real life, there is no final answer; the end of the narration is the beginning of a new quest. And whoever in the audience lived those times will remember those inner conflicts, with the alternation of expectation, illusion, disillusionment and a feeling of defeat. Like a reopened wound, the past comes back to our lives from the safety of oblivion.

This theatrical act derives from—or, better, is the evolution of—a live TV performance filmed at the Fori Imperiali in Rome, and broadcast by Italian State TV in 1998. From my recollection, the television performance can be considered a prototype that shared concepts, ideas, and even part of the staging but never achieved the same level of passion and participation as the theatrical version.

Even though the text and structure of the original performance have not undergone major changes, the final effect is quite different. New ideas are similar to rocks in a stream: time and repetition will smooth them the same way running water polishes the rocks and turns them into shiny stones. Repetition improves timing, enhances and clarifies detail, strengthens vision. We can say that in both performances the driver is emotion, but while in the theatrical version the result is achieved through intimacy and participation, the TV version relied more on pathos and intensity.

The theatrical version is emotionally superior. There are objective reasons that justify this perception. In theater the actor can "bathe" in his audience, but in television the camera will always "frame" the acting and create an unnatural separation between actor and audience. In theater we can share the sense of our feelings as parts of a greater audience, while when watching television we feel more like witnesses or bystanders.

But the emotional superiority of the theatrical performance is also dictated by ambience. In theater, the minimalist setting with a bare stage and dimmed lights favors identification with the narrator and participation in his stories. In television, the grand setting of the Fori Imperiali took the mind of the viewer back to the great orators of the ancient past and the feeling of tragedy prevailed over the feelings of doubt and inner conflict.

In the end, time has added to the emotional power of the performance rather than taking from it. The story—an amazing combination of history and daily stories magnificently brought to life on stage by Marco Baliani—suddenly becomes present again. The burden of elapsed years and diverse experiences which had dimmed the memory gets wiped away by the strength of words and emotions. The past comes back stronger, more vivid than ever.

And it is a mixture of perception, meditation, understanding and uneasiness for everybody. The ones who were there at the time will remember and find again their doubts, unresolved conflict, and search for identity. But the words of Marco Baliani will also permanently impress on the young—the ones who were not there yet—the picture of a decaying society and a sense of impotence over the impossibility of ever reaching the truth.

Marco Bendin
Independent software engineer
Chicago, Illinois

Reviews: New York University, Performance at Casa Zerilli-Marimò, New York (May 7, 2009) and St. John's University, Roundtable Discussion, "Resistere narrando," American Association of Italian Studies, New York (May 9, 2009)

Marco Baliani's performance of his one-man play *Body of State* is a unique kind of theatrical experience that is situated at the intersection of history and memory, public commemoration and private conflict. Let's call it, for now, a "theatre of memoir" that draws its enormous force from the ability to build on the authenticity and authority of its protagonist (a witness to history) who literally performs memory—its difficulties, its traumatic structures, the necessity of a willing audience of interlocutors—both for a collectivity (the audience) and collectively (in a uniquely occurring union with that same audience).

Because I'm so interested in the discrete singularity of any performance's chemical reaction with its audience, the question that struck me most insistently as I sat in the audience at the Casa Zerilli-Marimò was "What does it mean to perform this particular memory in the US, to a group of expatriate Italians, academic Italianists and students of Italian?" Any personal evocation of the years of lead aims to teach its audience something about the very chaotic years of open revolt and violent ideological turmoil, and, one would assume, their effect on our contemporary lives. In other words, this play would have a didactic and an ethical purpose no matter the audience; it's enough to consider Baliani's insistence on what he would and would not like to, what he could, and what he must "raccontar[ci] stasera" (tell us this evening). But unlike the implicit theatrical dialogue between Baliani and an Italian audience, the "conversation" happening on US soil must be a very different one. From the responses, comments, and questions of this particular audience, the function seems to have been a real thinking through of one person's struggle within and against the political currents of his day, but from a distance (especially palpable in the expatriate segment of the audience) that goes beyond the temporal divide Baliani underscores to his Italian audiences. Baliani's set and performance (such as the running self-commentary mentioned above) carry an undercurrent of meta-theatricality, as does the attention paid to the relationship between theater and political activism. This is true not just of the period represented in Baliani's monologue—about which Baliani remembers that he had turned to theatre from revolutionary politics well before the kidnapping and murder of Aldo Moro—but in the here and now, where it is clear that Baliani's mode of engaging with politics and ideological struggle is grounded in a grassroots-based theater of historical and personal awareness.

The post-show Q & A called to mind the "Playback" mode of improvisational theatre developed in New York in the 1970s, which solicits audience requests before performing scenarios, situations, dialogues on a given topic. In the context of my own teaching, I've taken Holocaust Literature students to see the Pittsburgh Playback Theatre group work with survivors and survivors' children; it's a collective and improvisational theatrical process that underscores and, well, dramatizes, the give and take that is always implicit between actors and audience. It also breaks down the fourth wall of theatre, not in any strictly Pirandellian sense, but rather by making visible and explicit the extent to which the audience guides and shapes the performance, and at the same time the extent to which the actors' performance aims to capture a certain audience with strategies that are specific to that audience, and indeed depends on the audience's demands and needs in order to shape his/her performance. It's also a kind of collective therapy; I think the element of the Q & A format at the end of Baliani's performance at NYU's Casa Zerilli-Marimò reproduced this therapeutic element of Playback Theatre in that the spectators were able to identify with various aspects of Baliani's reflective performance or experience, or both. Moreover, the powerful nature of audience comments—on everything from Italian political apathy to the importance of collective, public experiences in modern life—provided their own kind of collective theatricalization of the memorialization of the struggles (individual and collective alike) of the years of lead. I would argue further that this collection of written responses to the performance in the present volume constitutes an extension of this, producing a kind of multi-faceted hypertext for re-evoking the experience of Baliani's one-man show.

The idea of providing a full contextualization for this experience is a natural one in a format (both the theatrical memoir and the Q & A that followed) where the performance and its audience are so intertwined and so jointly responsible for the success of the piece's ethical and didactic mission. Baliani's piece has a strong confessional undercurrent that grants the narration an "I was there" authenticity, but also functions as a therapeutic theatrical "dialogue" (whose potential is realized in the Q & A) whereby the audience become witnesses to a history whose intensely personal conflicts are performed on the stage in front of us. Thus, through the intermingling of personal, viscerally evoked memory (of rage, of euphoria, even of unrequited love) and public documentation (headlines from *L'Unità* and *Il Manifesto*, Pasolini quotes), Baliani through his performance of conflict transforms himself into a kind of everyman, a screen onto which the audience, in turn, could project their own tensions, more or less related to the specific historical framework of *Body of State*. This is nowhere more powerful than in the final sequence of the play, when Baliani recounts the burning of his old address book—in a gesture that evokes his earlier refusal to submit to a radical and violent *clandestinità*—laying bare his vulnerability to very normal fears and flaws. He also shows in this gesture that the very performance we were all witnessing had the power to reverse even the most profound desire to disown his own story, his own history, and those of his closest friends.

To return to my initial question: what does it mean to tell this story to this sort of audience, and what is the ethical impact of Baliani's performance on an American (albeit Italophile) audience whose relationship to the years of lead is decidedly displaced in comparison to an Italian audience? Baliani's explicit reflections on his own private memory, his ability to dramatically re-enact a moment and then almost simultaneously step away from it to see it with today's eyes, result in a theatrical experience that is as much process as product, a performance of working through private memory that both reproduces the process on stage and demonstrates that process—as collective, public endeavor—for its audience.

Lina Insana
University of Pittsburgh

Marco Baliani's Corpo di Stato

I was privileged to be among the spectators of *Body of State: The Moro Affair, a Nation Divided*, created and performed by Marco Baliani and directed by Maria Maglietta at the Casa Italiana Zerilli-Marimò in New York on May 7, 2009. We were an "interested" audience, including participants who attended the annual conference of the American Association for Italian Studies held in New York that weekend and members of the Casa Italiana. The auditorium was packed: from the moment that Marco Baliani began his monologue we were mesmerized for an hour.

Marco Baliani recounts the story of how his generation experienced a decade of turmoil in Italy from the student protests of 1968 to the kidnapping and murder of Aldo Moro in 1978. Baliani offers us his personal testimony to the events of those years, events that we are drawn into directly through his first person narrative and the use of present tense as well as the projection of actual documentary footage from the period in question. Baliani not only recounts the events and the diverse emotions felt by his generation, he succeeds in explaining to the audience how these events could have happened. Thus, we are drawn into the struggle and are able to understand how the desire to form a better Italian society turned from protest to violence.

Baliani begins his story with Valle Giulia and the occupation of the Department of Architecture at the University of Rome in 1973. The student protests were no longer peaceful. Students and police now clashed openly with each other. At the time Baliani was participating in musical theatrical performances with a political intent. At this point Baliani flashes ahead to Aldo Moro's murder on May 9, 1978, in Rome as well as Peppino Impastato's murder on the same day in Sicily. Baliani recounts the "facts" of both events, but he does so as if he and we were witnessing them directly, though 31 years have passed. Spectators feel his emotions, from excitement to devastation throughout the performance.

Baliani recounts his initial reaction to the news of Aldo Moro's kidnapping: euphoria and praise, not shock and contempt. But then he listens to the reactions of others in the market: fear of a state reprisal, offers of sacrifices of other political figures, and a woman's chagrin over the deaths of Moro's police escorts. His elation was gone by evening.

Baliani tells the audience that his story could be told from another perspective, that of a generational conflict between fathers and sons, two walls up against each other. Police invaded student manifestations; students responded with open warfare. The images that are intertwined with Baliani's tales of specific encounters remind us of Tano D'Amico's photographs during these years: images of police in helmets, young protesters covered with bandanas, and fists raised.[4]

In his monologue Baliani confronts the question that everyone asks about this sad period: When did the conflict become out of control? How else was his generation supposed to respond to the massacre of Piazza Fontana? But Baliani never accepted the inevitable conclusion that armed resistance and revolutionary struggle could manifest itself in the kidnapping and murder of a statesman. After the funerals of Aldo Moro's bodyguards, Baliani reflects back on the rapid escalation of warfare: how his generation had progressed from meetings to organized protests, to how to defend themselves with arms, and finally to accept the call to go into hiding and kill without questioning.

Baliani does not offer solutions or answers to this dark era of terrorism in Italy. The audience is left with the task of interpretation 31 years later. Through Baliani's oral narration, the story becomes ours, and it becomes a true story.

The American edition in translation of *Body of State: The Moro Affair, a Nation Divided* is a noteworthy contribution to Italian Studies and fills a major gap in providing accessible testimony for our students.

Patricia Di Silvio
Tufts University

Body of State: *A Personal Matter*

Who is Aldo Moro? Or, better, what does the figure of Aldo Moro represent for you? This query resonated in *Body of State*. Who was Aldo Moro for me? I was not there. I was too young to even realize what was happening. Marco Baliani's play, therefore, did not speak to my memory, but gave me the possibility to become part of the collective memory of that period, handing me the images and the words necessary to talk about it and to be an active agent in its construction. Who was Aldo Moro for me, then? My response to this crucial question will probably echo that of many people of my age, with whom I share the feeling of a strong connection with "Il caso Moro" [The Moro Affair]. Even though I was only three years old on May 9, 1978, the events around Moro's kidnapping and murder have resounded in my brain for my whole life. The figure of Moro has indeed been a ghostly presence for me, alive in the memories of my parents, portrayed in history books, or represented on TV. He was the emblem of the ambiguity of the period, a generational divider: Baliani's monologue in theory divides me from that generation but in facts he brings me closer to it.

A more concrete connection I have with the play *Body of State* dates back to the spring of 2005, when I was still a graduate student at the University of Pennsylvania. During that semester, I served as a teaching assistant for an advanced course in Italian play production, led by Nicoletta Marini-Maio. Marco Baliani's *Body of State* was one of the course's primary texts, and, integrated with various others, it helped give life to the original play production of *Antigoni*. With that background still fresh in my mind, I attended Baliani's performance of his play at the Casa Italiana Zerilli-Marimò (New York University) May 7, 2009. Without a doubt, both experiences enriched me personally and professionally, giving me the unique occasion to be simultaneously backstage, on stage and a member of the public.

At the University of Pennsylvania, during the course of one semester, Nicoletta and I guided students in each stage of an original play production: preparing background reading materials, adapting scripts, rehearsing, and putting the play on stage. Since we were in need of extras, I also briefly acted in the play as Paola, an imagined friend of the narrator; my role was to agree with him about not joining the extreme activists of the Red Brigades. On that occasion, I experienced firsthand how such a course, which integrates theory with practice, can motivate students. But what struck me in particular is the degree to which a course based on critical background and historical materials, a course about Aldo Moro, could do so. I strongly believe that studying the historical facts at the base of a play production acted as a unique inspiration for the students on a personal level. I was especially amazed by the way each student, without exception, in spite of having no prior knowledge of the issue, reacted to it emotionally, bringing it close to his/her own experiences. Their performance was memorable, and the common reaction of the public (or those members of Italian heritage) was very personal. I heard many saying: "I remember that day as if it were yesterday."

This was not much different from the reaction I had when watching the monologue *Body of State* for the first time at the Casa Italiana Zerilli-Marimò in New York City. On that stage, Marco Baliani was talking to me personally. I felt intimately connected to him as if I were his immediate interlocutor, as if I had been an eyewitness to the events of Moro's death and could rely on him on some personal level. What was I doing on that day? How did that day affect my life? Of course I can't remember, but Baliani provided me with the memories, the words, and the images that I felt like I should have, if I want to play a part in the collective remembering and explaining the facts that have been going on since 1978. The images of that event are now alive in my mind, especially the Renault 4 with its vivid red trunk open, and they talk to my memory as if I had personally *seen* the events. What I know for sure, is that the memory of someone else—my parents, the media—had influenced me as a person, the way I look at and evaluate things in general, and politics in particular. Now, Marco offered me the generational memory I had already wanted to share, and of what I had only read and thought about.

Furthermore, Baliani's monologue activated my memory of another generational divider, another influential yet controversial figure of the period whose life was completely devoted to making a difference, and who is also significant for my personal academic path: Pier Paolo Pasolini. The grey zone Baliani describes, a condition of being "Neither with the Red Brigades, nor with the State," is sometimes connected with Leonardo Sciascia's critical neutrality. To me, however, it recalled the excruciating self-exploration of Pasolini's "Ashes of Gramsci," his being "With you and against you." His "scandal of self-contradiction" of being "with you in heart,/in the light, against you in visceral darkness" describes a feeling felt by many at that time, a feeling that many still feel considering the contemporary political scenario. Pasolini had a unique position in the panorama of the late 1960s and 1970s, inasmuch as he was very polemical with the student movement. He aroused big controversy with his poem "Il PCI ai giovani!," which accused the students [of being] "papa's children" fighting against the real proletarians—that is, the police. Pasolini and Baliani, nevertheless, are both outsiders, controversial, and provocative. They both urge the public to face uncomfortable issues. They present such issues in all their problematic stances, without urging to take sides, rather reflecting on the impossibility of doing so. They both engage in the representation of a difficult time with all its contradictions, and the public of today recognizes its topicality.

Who was Aldo Moro, then? Maybe it would be better to ask: Who is Aldo Moro today? He is an emblem of a compromise, a figure of a past that still interests many, and that Marco Baliani's monologue brings closer to us in the present, talking to each one of us personally, going beyond the historical event of Moro's death to speak about the way power and politics intermingle, affecting us all.

Silvia Carlorosi
Department of French and Italian
University of Maryland

Watching Marco Baliani's Body of State

As I watched *Body of State* at the Casa Italiana Zerilli-Marimò in May I started thinking that I was not even ten when the occupation of the School of Architecture at Valle Giulia took place, and when Marco Baliani, as he told us, started acting and moving in the direction of the politically engaged theater that more than 35 years later he was performing for us. And it particularly struck me to learn, right at the beginning, that one of Baliani's more intransigent comrades had derisively labeled him and his fellow players as "actors," as opposed to true "comrades," in order to discredit them in the eyes of their audience, as if a supposedly just and common cause could not be served by acting, as if that reality could be lived but not represented on stage, let alone be made fun of. Also especially telling, I found, was the story of the assembly in which the majority of the attendees ended up agreeing with the skillful orator comrade Riccardo that the times had changed and now called for a new form of political participation, one that required taking up arms and clandestine life. Sympathetic as I was towards Baliani's friends who were unjustly killed or imprisoned, and with the youthful, perhaps exaggerated enthusiasm of their egalitarian dreams, I was also thinking that those committed young men and women must have been terribly serious, and also unbearably self-righteous. Yet I know that the stories that Baliani re-enacted for us make up a bulky part of the history of his generation. The contemporary photographs, magnified and projected on a screen, the songs, the documentary footage, the news reports, and the recording of the telephone call announcing where Moro's dead body could be found—all played as short intermissions to Baliani's monologue—were there to reinforce the sense of reality that pervaded his performance. The circumstantial, historical backdrop of the "Moro Affair" was vividly brought back to our eyes, and in the end it is irrelevant if the actor himself threw a Molotov cocktail at the police during a political demonstration-turned-riot, or if he really had Peppino Impastato's number in his own address book. The personal (real or invented) and the historical events that Baliani so convincingly juxtaposed in his monologue transformed his performance into more than a theatrical representation. Impersonating a plausible, previous version of himself, Baliani did not even seem to be an actor anymore: he suddenly became an eyewitness, standing in front of a jury made up of people who were not there at the time and who were now called upon to reach some sort of verdict in the trial of a generation—for me, the generation of an elder brother. Listening to Baliani tell his stories I again realized how clearly many of his friends and comrades seemed to be completely unaware that the policemen with whom they were fighting in the streets were just as young as they were. In fact, those policemen, as Pasolini pointed out, were much more the expression of the proletariat than Baliani and his fellow students thought themselves to be, and yet were portrayed as nothing but instruments of the enemy, an evil power that had to be defeated. I was fifteen when Aldo Moro was kidnapped and killed. I had been born and was living in a very small, sleepy country town in northern Italy, and there we felt the effects of those traumatic days only through what we saw on TV, or read in the newspapers. There were no demonstrations in my area, no riots with the police, and no friends arrested or killed, not even distant acquaintances. As I had often thought years later, I had also been born too late and too far from the center of the universe to partake in the idealism, the enthusiasm, the sense of liberation, the joyful get-togethers of young people sharing a common, great dream, as Baliani said in the close of his monologue. Yet, last May, while watching his performance here in the U.S., at a relatively safe distance from the country Italy has become, another thought crossed my mind: the political power, both the government and the opposition, is now wielded by people who were young with Baliani. Many who back then were militants in his same political movement are now fervent supporters of Berlusconi's coalition with their old enemies, and post-Fascists, post–Christian Democrats as well as post-Communists are now the ones in charge. Maybe, as Baliani claimed, the idealistic movement that he was part of committed suicide in the days of the "Moro Affair," their dreams of justice and social change shattered in the face of a reality that the historians have not yet completely fathomed and accurately portrayed. And the story of Peppino Impastato, about whom most of us only learned many years after his murder, is there to confirm this, along with the dead at Piazza Fontana, at Ustica, and at the Bologna train station, and the many other Italian "mysteries."[5] Maybe Aldo Moro wanted changes in the nature of the power that he had long represented, and for this had to be sacrificed by that very same power; maybe his assassins had once been true comrades who had started making unforgivable mistakes, and maybe a young idealistic leftist could not be on the side of the State of the Honorable Giulio Andreotti just as he could not be with the Red Brigades. I asked myself what I would have done had I been in Baliani's shoes. And my answer was that I probably would have done the same thing as he did: keep acting, because, of all the possible dreams of justice, one within reach is the illusion of reality that the theater recreates for us through the body of an actor, a very good actor like Marco Baliani.

Antonello Borra
Italian Studies
University of Vermont

"Ma il cielo è sempre più blu"

I saw Marco Baliani perform *Body of State* at the Casa Italiana Zerilli-Marimò in New York May 7, 2009, as part of the program of the annual American Association for Italian Studies conference. I had not previously seen the show on TV, but I had read the script of the play published in 2003, and was very moved by the text and the stories that it told. Watching, and especially listening to Baliani's performance on stage added a "live" albeit falsely immediate dimension, since theatre is always a mediation that no script can reproduce. The play deals with the kidnapping and assassination of Christian Democrat leader Aldo Moro on the part of the extreme leftist organization Red Brigades in 1978, an event that scars the Italian nation to these days.

However, my interest and fascination were aroused less by the narration of this overarching historical event than by the story of Marco, his friends, and his generation, and not simply because we find out where they were when history happened; rather, because of their own histories in those years, the 1970s. For me, it was not so much Moro's "body" that was evoked in Baliani's performance, but through the actor's "body" as the sole presence on the stage, it was metaphorically the body of an entire generation that his theatre so vividly captured. Perhaps "corpi di stato" [bodies of state] is a more fitting description for the story that we are told, for it was an entire generation, an exceptionally creative, inventive, and rebellious one, that was truncated by the murder of Moro, and the subsequent labeling of the 1970s as years of lead, including their equation with terrorism. Terrorism was an aspect of those years, but by no means the only one, and to continue to refer to that period simply in those terms is to miss the point entirely; it is to deny to new generations the potential that was unveiled then and that is relevant to these days: the power of words, of language to change society.

It is no accident that Baliani's performance begins much earlier than Moro's death. It opens in 1973 at the Facoltà di Architettura in Valle Giulia, Rome, which had been occupied as part of a nationwide students' movement dating back to the previous decade and demanding a complete overhaul of the educational system. Students were reclaiming access to higher education for all, availability of resources, houses, job positions and transparency in their allocation. In short, these students were questioning authority, its legitimacy and its location. Their motto was RIPRENDIAMOCI LA CITTÀ [let's take back the city]. Baliani tells his audience that it is in this politicized climate of self-organized workshops, collective participation and self-determination that his involvement with theatre started. In addition to Dario Fo's regular visits, it is the way the students themselves take control of the space of the university and of the knowledge that is supposedly being passed down that is significant. Baliani recounts that he and a group of other students often improvised performances, experimenting with different media, visual arts and music. They used histrionics to address current issues and enacted playful takes on established traditions and symbols: "è un teatro rozzo, semplice, tutto politico" [it is a rugged, simple, and completely political theatre].

These same qualities have remained in this play and constitute its strengths. In his North American tour, Baliani interspersed his monologue with original footage and music of those years to re-create the atmosphere of tension, protest, but also anticipation and excitement at the prospect of a new and more just world for all. The horizons of this movement were, in fact, limitless, they dreamt of the global, but paid attention to the local, so much so that one of the pamphlets they produced, Baliani tells us, was entitled *Da Woodstock a Mirafiori* [*From Woodstock to Mirafiori*], the well-known FIAT plant in Turin. In this respect, it was the use of certain songs during his performance that stuck with me well after it ended. In particular, Baliani chose to play "Ma il cielo è sempre più blu" by the Calabrian-born singer songwriter Rino Gaetano, an ironic and satirical song, full of pungency, provocation, and sarcasm at the false optimism of politicians which in many ways is still relevant today even though it grew out of the socio-political context of the 1970s. Manipulating language and drawing from nonsense and nursery rhymes Gaetano sings an entire song depicting an Italy not too distant from our own today:

> Chi vive in baracca, chi suda il salario
> Chi ama l'amore e i sogni di gloria
> Chi ruba pensioni, chi ha scarsa memoria
> Chi mangia una volta, chi tira al bersaglio
> Chi vuole l'aumento, chi gioca a Sanremo
> [. . .] na na na na na na na na na
> Ma il cielo è sempre più blu uh uh, uh uh,
> ma il cielo è sempre più blu uh uh, uh uh
> [Those who live in a dump, those who sweat for their salary
> Those who love love and dreams of glory
> Those who steal pensions, those who have short memory

Those who eat only once, those who target-shoot
Those who want a wage rise, those who gamble in Sanremo
[. . .] na na na na na na na na na
But the sky is always bluer uh uh, uh uh,
But the sky is always bluer uh uh, uh uh]

Likewise, Baliani concludes his performance with *Luglio, agosto, settembre (nero)*, a song by the 1970s experimental progressive rock band Area, one of the most innovative and revolutionary groups of their generation focused on exploring the utopian potential of music and blurring the boundaries between art and life.

Through the story of his first acting experiences and the use of specific songs, Baliani signaled the rebelliousness and protest of the youth of the 1970s, as well as the need for renewal and the desire for change in the arts as much as in society that can still be a veritable inspiration for today's younger generations. After all Baliani's theater—only apparently focused on the individual "I"—has strived to appeal precisely to aurality in its narrative underpinnings.

Clarissa Clò
Department of European Studies
San Diego State University

Culturemes and Doubts: Sallies around Baliani's Body of State

At St. John's University in New York, where the annual American Association of Italian Studies conference was held, a group of people was still gathered after the Round Table with Marco Baliani, talking about his show and his reflections on theater and society. Among others, there was a young scholar with a fine *cursus studiorum*—excellent college studies in Italy and a Ph.D. in an Ivy League University on the East Coast. Out of the blue, the young scholar took the center of the unplanned stage with one of those very strange and categorical declarations which often leave the auditors speechless (and embarrass the one pronouncing them). "Baliani's show on Moro was great, but the English subtitles were appalling," she said haughtily. Needless to say, one of the translators of those very subtitles was also present in our little group, and the young scholar had no idea he was there. Since I know him very well and know how seriously and skillfully he works, I felt sorry and turned red. Others in the group knew the translator as well, and an uncomfortable silence settled on our little circle. Without thinking, I stepped into the silence and introduced the author of such a supposed blasphemous iniquity to the young scholar. I also felt entitled to disagree publicly with her absolute and narrow critique. I let the reader imagine how embarrassed the (by now) poor young scholar was. It was her turn to turn red. She apologized and tried to justify herself by saying that it was more a superficial impression than anything else, and that what really annoyed her were the inacceptable translations of three words: "clandestinità," "fuorisede," "baroni."

To crucify a fifty-minute translation for the possible inadequacy of three words is discomforting to say the least, and even more so if referred to a show centered on the virtue of doubt, on questioning arrogant faith in absolute truths, on generational and political certainties. But I'll come back to this later on. For now I would like to linger a little more on the translation process, and on the attitude we should have when we face the problem of evaluating a translation. As modern translation studies always remind us, we never translate word by word, or sentence by sentence, but always text by text; and that we never translate from one language to another, but from a culture to another one. If you want your evaluation of a translation to be useful and not just an impulsive reaction, it will have to take into consideration not a single word, but the text as a complex structure made of words, rhythms, silences etc.; not two languages but two cultures. Antoine Berman, one of the more interesting translations studies scholars, devoted a fine essay to this problem (*Le proget d'une critique "productive"* in *Pour une critique des traductions: John Donne* [Paris, Gallimard, 1995]), which I recommend with pleasure to the young Italian scholar and to whoever cares about issues of translation, one of the most crucial activities today.

But the anecdote allows me to deal directly with a few linguistic aspects of Baliani's theatrical work. *Body of State* is a tragedy. The storyteller could have chosen a high, "illustre" style (to use Dante's word) or an aseptic one, detached in time and space, with a sort of universal lexicon, as in Beckett's absurd tragedies or in Kafka stories. Baliani's text instead is stuffed with hot expressions and words. They could be defined "affective words," highly evocative because referring to a specific historical and cultural setting. They are expressions strongly related to the collective imagination of a particular culture and only that culture. They are usually defined by the word "cultureme." These elements raise particular problems in the process of translating, but when they are translated with wit and wisdom, they force us to enter into the mental and cultural world of the others, they force us not to completely domesticate the other text, not to entirely subdue the translated text to target cultures. Culturemes are often found in advertisements. The so-called Italian "teatro di narrazione" also uses them abundantly, both as a poetic choice and due to its specific nature, i.e., of being a narrative monologue intentionally addressed to a wide and variously educated audience. One of the problems in translating another tragic theatrical narration, *The Story of Vajont* (edited by Thomas Simpson [Boca Raton, FL: Bordighera Press, 2000]), was the rendering in English of expressions such as "l'elmetto Moplen" or "il trench del tenente Sheridan," objects used by Marco Paolini to sketch one of the protagonists of his historical theatrical piece. These two objects are full of resonances, but they can only be perceived by someone who lived in Italy in the 1960s, and spent part of his life watching television and *Carosello* (a funny show of advertisements broadcast every night before children's bedtime and followed with ritualistic devotion by millions of Italian families). A culturally homogeneous community immediately grasps the strength of these images, what they directly or allusively mean. These are the kind of expressions that can recreate a situation deeply lived and experienced. Whoever was, as was I, a university student at the time of Moro's kidnapping, and was *engagé* in changing the world, as was almost everybody at that time in Italy, would find himself plunged during Baliani's monologue into a solid and homogeneous universe made of culturemes. Every object (from the kind of car to the name of a gun), every quotation (from song lyrics to the slogans yelled at political rallies) is there to recreate that historical moment for the audience. It is necessarily difficult to transpose that avalanche of information and feeling into a synthetic sentence, as must be done with subtitles in cinema and theater. The three words that the young scholar reckoned as unbearably bad translations are part of the style of the storyteller Baliani. They are culturally specific words and therefore hard to translate. But since a translation had to be done anyway, the choices were "Outsider," "Underground," and "Fat cat," for "Fuorisede," "Clandestinità," and "Barone."

It could be interesting to try to comprehend the reasons that led the translator to choose these solutions, and also to understand what they imply. In the seventies in Italy, not many students left their family houses to go far away for their university education. The "fuorisede" were mostly young students from the south enrolled in state universities far from home, who lived in crowded, expensive, tiny apartments shared with other "fuorisede," or off campus. Living on a very tight budget, many worked part-time jobs. Most regular students, on the other hand, attended university near their family home and thereby at the expense of their families. In America, by contrast, it is a diffuse cultural habit to choose a university far from home as a first symbolic sign of independence and exit from "a condition of minority." To live on campus in the States is normal; to be a student "fuorisede" in Italy 30 years ago was less normal. The expression "fuorisede" brings with it the idea of economic unsteadiness but at the same time of independence from the family compared to the greater mass of students. In those years, such independence meant, for many, the possibility to devote themselves fulltime to political activism. The English word chosen to render such a complex cultureme (i.e., "Outsider") is absolutely reasonable and perhaps the only one that can express that complicated word in an economical way. But it raises a secondary and, in a way, unpredictable problem: "Outsider" is a foreignism commonly used in Italian, but with the specific meaning (very often negative) of someone who is excluded, or, in the language of sport, someone who wins unexpectedly. It happens very often that the same word used in two different languages/cultures has different meanings. The same could be said for the word "Underground" (used to translate "clandestinità"). In this case also the term is a foreignism commonly used in Italian, but its semantic range (related mostly to the underground culture of the Beats) is more limited compared to the variety of meanings it has in English. Very few in Italy would use that term for the partisans of World War II, for example. Our perception of its usage in the original language is necessarily restrained, or at least conditioned, by our previous familiarity with the same word used in a different linguistic *milieu*. The nature of the problem for the third word the young scholar pointed out is different. "Barone" is a way of defining a very powerful professor. In Italy in the 1970s (but things have not changed), a "barone" was like a despot who could determine quite arbitrarily the career (and consequently life) of the students. Academia in Italy recalls the medieval feudal system, with the students as the oppressed glebe and the full professors, often exploiters and dictators, at the spire of the pyramid. Since the young scholar of the anecdote had been oppressed by her "barone" in Italy, and forced to leave the country if she wanted to continue her career in literary studies, she felt that the image of a "fat cat" was not strong enough, not mean enough.[6] We are here still in the realm of culturemes, but with a secondary problem of figurative language. "Fat cat" certainly evokes a visual image, perhaps suggesting idleness and passivity, but in English it is used as a *cliché* and therefore culturally and historically rooted in that linguistic *milieu*, whereas for a foreigner it is mostly just an image. Similarly, the word "barone" for a young lecturer in Italy is much more meaningful that the simple metaphoric use of the term "barone."

Briefly, the anecdote allows me to emphasize a basic element in Baliani's style—that is, the use of a lexicon anthropologically rooted deep in the Italian culture described in his theatrical works—and also to offer a little advice to whoever wants to judge a translation. My advice is: use caution, doubt everything, use the same doubt that resonates so clearly in Baliani's tragic monologue on Moro. We are often as imprisoned in our linguistic certainties as the generation that Baliani depicts in *Body of State* was imprisoned in its historical and ideological certainties.

Speaking of advice and counsel, Walter Benjamin's pages devoted to Leskov, "The Art of the Storyteller" (as the "man who has counsel—*Rat* in German—for his readers"), come to mind. In the 1930s, Benjamin believed, the art of storytelling was declining. It was ever more difficult to meet someone able to tell a tale properly: "It is as if something that seemed inalienable to us, the securest among our possessions, were taken from us: the ability to exchange experiences."[7]

To recount an experience is not the same as to inform in a superficial way or as newspapers do. There is a fundamental difference between the two ways of telling stories. Narration is deeply rooted in the spirit of a people, of a country in a certain time and space, and lives within a shared experience. Information, instead, is concerned with every possible new event, leaving readers or viewers paradoxically "poor in noteworthy stories. This is because no event any longer comes to us without already being shot through with explanation."[8] The news, with its presumed objectivity, has taken the place of narration, full of life and subjectivity, of wisdom and imagination.

> Storytelling . . . does not aim to convey the pure essence of the thing, like information or a report. It sinks the thing into the life of a storyteller, in order to bring it out of him again. Thus traces of the storyteller cling to the story the way that the handprints of the potter cling to the clay vessel. Storytellers tend to begin their story with a presentation of the circumstances in which they themselves learned of what is to follow, or they simply pass it off as their own experience.[9]

To be able to recount a place, an object, a state of being, one needs to have a deep knowledge of that place, object, and state, and also must master perfectly the specific language of that situation, the culturemes. The teller needs to know the experience from the inside, but in the same time must see it from a distance, so as to give back to the listener both its inside flavor and its external profile. To be deeply inside the situation, to recount it "live," as journalists or blog writers often do, might give back the freshness and immediacy of the experience, but not the complexity of the situation. To be happily in love or undergo a devastating mental crisis or be witness of a historical event, as Moro's kidnapping was, is not enough to make you able to narrate that experience. Maybe Wordsworth and Leopardi were not wrong when they recommended letting time pass, to arrive at a state of tranquility before writing lines about intense experiences that can trigger the thunderstorm of powerful feelings that the poet wants to recreate and recall.

In her introduction to *Tu che mi guardi, tu che mi racconti. Filosofia della narrazione* [*Relating Narratives: Storytelling and Selfhood*], Adriana Cavarero cites a story that Karen Blixen learnt when she was a child.[10] The story is about a man who, during a stormy night, has to leave his house to bolster the banks of a pond that threatens to overflow and destroy his home. He falls several times trying to find his way around the pond in the dark. The next morning the sun comes out again, and looking down at his house from the top of a hill, he sees that the footprints he left on the muddy ground during the night had marked out the profile of a huge stork. The image gives sense and unity to the action he took in a moment of crisis. Such unity was not planned, but is found after the action has taken place. This is Cavarero's comment:

> Like the drawing, the story comes after the events and actions, and it derives from them. Like the drawing seen only at sunrise from the perspective of someone looking down from above, the story can be told only from a posthumous perspective, by someone not part of the events. "When the drawing of my life will be complete, will I see, or will others see, a stork?" . . . The stork does not "do," but carries, transports, transmits. It is a storyteller, is not an author. Like Karen Blixen, the stork is a storyteller.[11]

According to Hannah Arendt, quoted by Cavarero in her piece on the Blixen tale, "Life cannot be lived as a story, because the story always comes after, it results—unpredictable and unmasterable, just like life is."[12] If the man had intentionally wanted to draw the profile of a stork, his story would not have been that of a man trying to save a pond, but the story of a man trying to draw a stork with his own footprints. The storyteller is the one who can see the profile.

With his theatrical monologue on the tragic and hectic days of Moro's murder, Baliani has clearly shown that he has the "view from above," the detachment necessary to see the profile—and in the profile you see Moro, his policemen, an eighteen-year-old killed by the police, and the politicians, and all the hesitations and fears and hopes. But at the same time he has deeply lived that experience, a necessary condition, according to Benjamin, of the real storyteller. The need to tell that story it not a mere psychoanalytical outburst, nor—still worse—a narcissistic reverie on the way we were, but the achievement of counsel, of advice. And the advice that arises from the emotions and the arguments filling the narrow scenic space is the admonition to doubt. Doubt about easy slogans, doubt whoever believes to have in hand the pen that can write history while we are still living it, doubt about the strong narratives or Lyotard's *grands récits*, the lenses through which everything is explained categorically and definitively. Baliani tells us about the tragic, confused, appalling days of the kidnapping of Moro from a different perspective, that is at the same time a bird's eye view and an intimate one, linguistically rich, emotionally involving, historically documented, with the controlled, unemphatic and problematic tone of wisdom.

Franco Nasi
Facoltà di Lettere e Filosofia
University of Modena and Reggio Emilia, Italy

Contributors to the Appendix

Nadja Aksamija, Wesleyan University
Perrin Allen, Dickinson College

Marco Bendin, Chicago
Paola Bonifazio, University of Texas at Austin
Antonello Borra, University of Vermont
Elena Brandano, Dickinson College
Silvia Carlorosi, University of Maryland
Lucie Carrara, Université Toulouse Le Mirail
Clarissa Clò, San Diego State University
Michael Dalton, Dickinson College
Dario Del Puppo, Trinity College
Luciano Di Palermo, Dickinson College
Patricia Di Silvio, Tufts University
Allyson Glazier, Dickinson College
Antonio González, Wesleyan University
Lina Insana, University of Pittsburgh
Brian Krussel, Dickinson College
Zoe Lutz, Dickinson College
Ian Andrew MacDonald, Dickinson College
Paola Morgavi, Northwestern University
Franco Nasi, University of Modena and Reggio Emilia
Chiara Olivi, Dickinson College
Sharon Perrone, Dickinson College
Colleen Ryan, Indiana University
Adele Sanna, University of Virginia
Genevieve Saul, Dickinson College
William Stowe, Wesleyan University
Brendan Stuart, Dickinson College
Pamela Tatge, Wesleyan University
Kelly Zwink, Dickinson College

Notes

1. See the introduction for an explanation of the "historic compromise" between Italy's Christian Democratic and Communist Parties.

2. For details about the Reale Law, please see the introduction.

3. For the *strategia della tensione*, or strategy of tension, and the bombings mentioned by the student, please see the introduction.

4. *Gli anni ribelli 1968–1980*, Tano D'Amico, *Storia fotografica della società italiana*, edited by Giovanni De Luna and Diego Mormorio (Rome: Editori Riuniti, 1998).

5. Editors' note: Italy's "mysteries," which, for example, writer and TV personality Carlo Lucarelli has popularized in his television and book series of the same name, include, in addition to Moro's assassination, Pier Paolo Pasolini's murder, Itavia Flight 870

shot down over Ustica in 1980, and the mysterious death of Wilma Montesi in 1953. See Carlo Lucarelli, *I casi di "Blu Notte"* (available on DVD) and published by Einaudi. On the Wilma Montesi mystery, see also Karen Pinkus, *The Montesi Scandal: The Death of Wilma Montesi and the Birth of the Paparazzi in Fellini's Rome* (Chicago: University of Chicago Press, 2003).

6. The rhyming "fat cat" was used to translate *barone* because both are pejorative terms used to describe individuals operating within a system in which they feed parasitically off the work of others. *Barone*, which smacks of "university don" in the British system, obviously implies a feudal arrangement, with the professor occupying the position of the landed baron and the student (or anyone who is not a professor) in the position of the serf. "Fat cat" usually refers to a capitalist who has profited from sketchy dealings and has grown fat from his feedings.

7. Walter Benjamin, *Illuminations*, edited by Hannah Arendt (New York: Schocken Books, 1968), 83.

8. Ibid., 89.

9. Ibid., 91–92.

10. Adriana Cavarero, *Tu che mi guardi, tu che mi racconti* (Milan: Feltrinelli, 1997).

11. Ibid., 8–9.

12. Ibid., 9.

Bibliography

Antonello, Pierpaolo, and Alan O'Leary, eds. *Imagining Terrorism: The Rhetoric and Representation of Political Violence*. Oxford: Legenda, 2009.

Augias, Corrado, and Vladimiro Polchi. *Aldo Moro. Una tragedia italiana*. Milano: Studio Teatro Piccolo, 2008.

Baliani, Marco. "Esperienza—tempo—verità: Un seminario sulla narrazione." In *La bottega dei narratori: Storie, laboratori e metodi di: Marco Baliani, Ascanio Celestini, Laura Curino, Marco Paolini, Gabriele Vacis*, edited by Gerardo Guccini. Rome: Dino Audino Editore, 2005.

———. *Ho cavalcato in groppa ad una sedia*. Pisa: Titivillus, 2010.

Baliani, Marco, and Remo Rostagno. *Kohlhaas*. Perugia: Futura, 2001.

Bartali, Roberto. "The Red Brigades and the Moro Kidnapping: Secrets and Lies." In *Speaking Out and Silencing: Culture, Society, and Politics in Italy in the 1970s*, edited by Anna Cento Bull and Adalgisa Giorgio. Oxford: Legenda, 2006.

Beckett, Samuel. *The Complete Short Prose, 1929–1989*. New York: Grove Press, 1995.

Bellocchio, Marco, dir. *Buongiorno, notte*. 2003 [movie].

Benedetti, Carla. "Free Italian Epic." http://www.ilprimoamore.com/testo_1376.html.

Benjamin, Walter. *Illuminations*. Edited by Hannah Arendt. New York: Schocken Books, 1968.

Bianconi, Giovanni. *Eseguendo la sentenza*. Turin: Einaudi, 2008.

Bloch, Marc. *Apologie pour l'histoire, ou, Métier d'historie*. Paris: A. Colin, 1993.

Boato, Marco. "Né con lo stato né con le BR: Si cerca di prendere l'iniziativa." *Lotta Continua*. March 18, 1978.

Boatti, Giorgio. *Piazza Fontana: 12 dicembre 1969: Il giorno dell'innocenza perduta*. Turin: Einaudi, 1999.

Brook, Peter. *The Shifting Point*. New York: Harper & Row, 1987.

Bruno, Giuliana. "The Body of Pasolini's Semiotics: A Sequel Twenty Years Later." In *Pier Paolo Pasolini: Contemporary Perspectives*, edited by Patrick Rumble and Bart Testa. Toronto: University of Toronto Press, 1994, 88–105.

Calvino, Italo. *The Path to the Spiders' Nest*. Translated by A. Colquhoun, revised by Martin McLaughlin. New York: HarperCollins, 2000.

———. *Romanzi e racconti*, 3 volumes. Edited by Milanini, Claudio, Mario Barenghi, and Bruno Falcetto. Milan: Mondadori, 1991–1994.

Calvino, Italo, ed. "Prezzemolina," in *Fiabe italiane raccolte e trascritte da Italo Calvino*. Turin: Einaudi, 1956.

Camus, Albert. *Between Hell and Reason: Essays from the Resistance Newspaper Combat, 1944–1947*. Edited and translated by Alexandre de Gramont. Middletown, CT: Wesleyan U P, 1991.

Cavarero, Adriana. *Tu che mi guardi, tu che mi racconti*. Milan: Feltrinelli, 1997.

Clementi, Marco. *La "pazzia" di Aldo Moro*. Milan: Rizzoli, 2008.

D'Amico, Tano. *Storia fotografica della società italiana*. Edited by Giovanni De Luna and Diego Mormorio. Rome: Editori Riuniti, 1998.

De Luna, Giovanni, and Diego Mormorio, eds. *Storia fotografica della società italiana*. Rome: Editori Riuniti, 1998.

Deleuze, Gilles. *The Fold, Liebniz, and the Baroque*. Foreword and translation by Tom Conley. Minneapolis: University of Minnesota Press, 1992.

Della Porta, Donatella. *Social Movements, Political Violence, and the State*. Cambridge: Cambridge University Press, 1995.

Drake, Richard. "The Aldo Moro Murder Case in Retrospect." *Journal of Cold War Studies* 8:2 (2006): 114–25.

Flamigni, Sergio. *Convergenze parallele: Le Brigate Rosse, i servizi segreti e il delitto Moro*. Milan: Kaos, 1998.

———. *La tela del ragno: Il delitto Moro*. 5th ed. Milan: Kaos, 2003.

Fo, Dario. *Manuale Minimo Dell'Attore*. Turin: Einaudi, 1987.

Ginsborg, Paul. *Storia d'Italia 1943–1996*. Turin: Einaudi, 1998.

Ginzburg, Carlo. *The Cheese and the Worms: The Cosmos of a Sixteenth Century Miller* Baltimore: Johns Hopkins University Press, 1980.

Glynn, Ruth. "Terrorism, a Female Malady." In *Terrorism, Italian Style: Representations of Political Violence in Contemporary Italian Cinema*, edited by Ruth Glynn, Giancarlo Lombardi and Alan O'Leary. London: IGRS Books, forthcoming.

Glynn, Ruth, and Giancarlo Lombardi, eds. *Re-membering Moro: The Cultural Legacy of the Kidnapping and Death of Aldo Moro*. Oxford: Legenda, forthcoming.

Gotor, Miguel. *Lettere dalla prigionia*. Edited by Aldo Moro. Turin: Einaudi, 2008.

Grassi, Stefano. *Il caso Moro: Un dizionario italiano*. Milan: Mondadori, 2008.

Jenkins, Ron. *Acrobats of the Soul: Comedy & Virtuosity in Contemporary American Theatre*. New York: Theater Communications Group, 1988.

———. *Artful Laughter*. New York: Aperture, 2001.

Kobialka, Michal. "Introduction." *Of Borders and Thresholds: Theater History, Practice and Theory*. Minneapolis: University of Minnesota Press, 1999.

Le Febvre, Lucien. *Le problème de l'incroyance au XVI siècle*. Lucien, Paris: Albin Michel, 1947.

Lepre, Aurelio. *Storia della Prima Repubblica: L'Italia dal 1944 al 1992*. Bologna: Il Mulino, 1993.

Lucarelli, Carlo. *Misteri d'Italia. I casi di Blu notte*. Turin: Einaudi, 2002.

Martone, Mario, dir. *Teatro di guerra*. Milan: Bompiani, 1998 [movie].

Mecchia, Giuseppina. "Moro's Body Between Enlightenment and PostModernism: Terror, Murder and Meaning in the Writings of Leonardo Sciascia and Jean Baudrillard." In *Terrorism, Italian Style: Representations of Political Violence in Contemporary Italian Cinema*, edited by Ruth Glynn, Giancarlo Lombardi, and Alan O'Leary. London: IGRS Books, forthcoming.

Nerenberg, Ellen. "To Strike at the Heart of State and Family: Gianni Amelio's *Colpire al Cuore*." In *Terrorism, Italian Style: Representations of Political Violence in Contemporary Italian Cinema*, edited by Ruth Glynn, Giancarlo Lombardi, and Alan O'Leary. London: IGRS Books, forthcoming.

Orton, Marie. "De-monstering the Myth of the Terrorist Woman: Faranda, Braghetti, and Mambro." *Romance Languages Annual* 16 (1998): 281–96.

Pasolini, Pier Paolo. "1 Febbraio 1975: L'articolo delle lucciole." In *Tutte le opere: Saggi sulla politica e sulla società*, edited by Walter Siti and Silvia De Laude, 404–11. Milan: Mondadori, 1999.

———. "Contro la televisione." In *Tutte le opere: Saggi sulla politica e sulla società*, edited by Walter Siti and Silvia De Laude. Milan: Mondadori, 1999.

———. *Lettere Luterane*. Turin: Einaudi, 1976.

———. "Manifesto." *Nuovi argomenti* 9 (1968): 6–22.

———. *Tutte le opere: Saggi sulla politica e sulla società*. Edited by Walter Siti and Silvia De Laude. Milan: Mondadori, 1999.

Pinkus, Karen. *The Montesi Scandal: The Death of Wilma Montesi and the Birth of the Paparazzi in Fellini's Rome*. Chicago: University of Chicago Press, 2003.

Sciascia, Leonardo. *L'Affaire Moro*. Piccola Biblioteca. 2nd edition. Milan: Adelphi, 1983.

———. *The Moro Affair and the Mystery of Majorana*. Translated by Sacha Rabinovitch. New York/Manchester, UK: Carcanet, 1987.

Socìetas Raffaello Sanzio. *Tragedia Endogonidia*. 2002–2004 [stage show].

Sofri, Adriano. *L'ombra di Moro*. Palermo: Sellerio, 1991.

Soriani, Simone. "Dario Fo, il teatro di narrazione, la nuova 'performance' epica: Per una genealogia d'un 'quasi-genere.'" *Forum Italicum* 39:2 (Fall 2005): 620–48.

Sorrentino, Paolo, dir. *Il Divo*. 2008 [movie].

Tassini, Eugenio, ed. *Aldo Moro: Ultimi scritti*. Casale Monferrato (AL): Piemme, 2003.

Tullio Giordana, Marco. *I cento passi*. 2000 [movie].

Wagner-Pacifici, Robin. *The Moro Morality Play: Terrorism as Social Drama*. Chicago: University of Chicago Press, 1986.

Watson, William Van. *Pier Paolo Pasolini and the Theater of the Word*. Ann Arbor: UMI Research Press, 1989.

Wu Ming. *New Italian Epic*. Turin: Einaudi, 2009.

Index

About the Translators

Nicoletta Marini-Maio is coeditor of the bilingual academic journal *Quaderni del '900*. With Colleen Ryan she has edited the volumes *Set the Stage! Teaching Italian through Theater, Theories, Methods, and Practices* (2010) and *Dramatic Interactions* (2011). She is currently completing a monograph on the representations of the 1978 abduction and assassination of Aldo Moro in film and theater. She holds degrees from the University of Perugia, the University of Rome, and the University of Pennsylvania. She is associate professor of Italian at Dickinson College.

Ellen Nerenberg is the author of *Prison Terms: Representing Confinement During and After Italian Fascism* (2001), winner of the Modern Language Association's Howard R. Marraro Prize. She served as coeditor of *Writing beyond Fascism: Cultural Resistance in the Life and Works of Alba de Cèspedes* (2000) and is the author of *Murder Made in Italy: Homicide, Media, and Contemporary Italian Culture* (2012). She holds degrees from Stanford University and the University of Chicago and is professor of Romance languages and literatures at Wesleyan University.

Thomas Simpson is the author of *Murder and Media in the New Rome: The Fadda Affair* (2010) and has contributed to *Suburbia: Teatro delle Albe* (2008), and *Pier Paolo Pasolini: In Living Memory*, edited by Ben Lawton and Maura Bergonzoni (2009). He has translated work by Pasolini and Giorgio Strehler for the *Performing Arts Journal* and *The Comic Mask in the Commedia dell'Arte* by Antonio Fava (2004) and *Mystery in Naples* by Ermanno Rea (2003). He received his PhD from the University of Chicago and teaches in the Department of French and Italian, at the Kaplan Institute for the Humanities, and in the Department of English at Northwestern University.